ST. KITTS & NEVIS TRAVEL GUIDE

Your Ultimate Companion for Exploring the Enchanting Islands with Expert Tips and Recommendations on Food and Lodging Options with a 7-Day Detailed Itinerary

ANDREA TOWNSON

CopyRight©2023 Andrea Townson

All Right Reserved

TABLE OF CONTENTS

TABLE OF CONTENTS 2

INTRODUCTION 7

WELCOME TO ST. KITTS AND NEVIS 10

CHAPTER ONE 15

CULTURE AND HISTORY 15
ST. KITTS AND NEVIS GEOGRAPHY 18
PEOPLE OF ST. KITTS AND NEVIS 21
RESOURCES AVAILABLE IN ST. KITTS AND NEVIS 24
GOVERNMENT 27
CHAPTER TWO 31
MAKING TRAVEL ARRANGEMENTS 31
WHEN SHOULD YOU VISIT 34
ACCESSING ST. KITTS AND NEVIS 35
HOW TO NAVIGATE ST. KITTS AND NEVIS 37
THE BEST PLACES TO STAY IN ST. KITTS AND NEVIS 39
WHAT TO BRING 42
ENTRY REQUIREMENTS AND VISAS 45
TOP TRAVEL BOOKING SITES 56

CHAPTER THREE 61

EXPLORING ST. KITTS 61
CITY OF THE CAPITAL: BASSETERRE 63
SQUARE INDEPENDENCE 66

NATIONAL GALLERY 69
NATIONAL PARK OF BRIMSTONE HILL FORTRESS 71
ROMNEY HOUSE 74
BAY OF FRIGATES 79
BEACHES AND WATER SPORTS 81
COCKLESHELL COVE 86
PUMP BAY ON SAINT KITTS 96
WILDLIFE AND NATURE 97
MOUNT NEVIS 110

CHAPTER FOUR **117**

EXPLORING NEVIS 117
THE HISTORIC CAPITAL OF CHARLESTOWN 120
THE COTTLE CHURCH 134
NEVIS' FORT CHARLES 136

CHAPTER FIVE **143**

ADVENTURES AND ACTIVITIES 143
NATURE AND HIKING TRAILS 145
FESTIVALS AND CULTURE IN THE COMMUNITY 148

CHAPTER SIX **151**

ENTERTAINMENT AND DINING 151
RESTAURANTS AND LOCAL CUISINE 154
CUISINE OF ST. KITTS 156
CUISINE FROM NEVIS 159
10 MUST-TRY LOCAL DELIGHTS 161
ST. KITTS MUST-TRY RESTAURANTS 163

Entertainment and Nightlife	165
Top Ten Pubs and Nightclubs	167
Live Music Venues	168
Shopping	170
Souvenirs and Gifts	173
Accessories and Fashion	174

CHAPTER SEVEN 177

Useful Information	177
Accommodation Options	179
Hotels and Resorts	181
Bed and Breakfasts	183
Vacation Rentals and Villas	184
Eco-Lodges and Camping	186

CHAPTER EIGHT 189

Tips for Safety and Security	189
Transportation by Public	191
Walking and Cycling	196
Services for Boats and Ferries	199
Traveling from St. Kitts to Nevis	202
Apps and Websites for Travel	205

CHAPTER NINE 209

Itinerary for 7 Days in St. Kitts and Nevis	209
Safety and Health	210
Medical Services and Facilities	212
Emergency Phone Numbers	217

INFORMATION ON THE WEATHER AND CLIMATE 220
TRAVEL INSURANCE 221

CONCLUSION 225

Andrea Townson

INTRODUCTION

I knew I was in for an incredible journey the moment I set foot on these twin islands. The smell of the tropics permeated the air, and the sound of the soft waves lapping against the coast entices me to continue exploring. The lively culture and kind residents welcomed me as I set out on my tour, making me feel like a member of their lively community.

Hiking through the lush jungles of St. Kitts, where each step took me further into a realm of unspoiled beauty, is one of my most treasured memories. My senses were awakened by the lush vegetation's symphony of natural sounds, which included the sounds of exotic birds and monkeys. As I climbed higher, I was overwhelmed by the breathtaking panoramas of the nearby islands and the Caribbean Sea. Realizing the incredible wonders that Mother Nature has to give, I was filled with awe and thankfulness at that very moment.

The adventure, however, didn't end there. For thrill lovers like me, St. Kitts & Nevis has a ton of exhilarating activities to choose from. I made the decision to go on a thrilling zipline tour that would take me above the treetops and give me a sight of the blue waters below. It was just thrilling to feel the wind blow into my face and to feel so free as I flew through the air. I was forced out of my comfort zone, and it was an exhilarating experience that gave me a strong sense of success.

Of course, my trip would not have been complete without learning more about the islands' rich past and cultural legacy. The unique history of St. Kitts is reflected in the island's attractive colonial buildings and historic sugar plantations. I started a historical tour, exploring the history as I walked through the capital city of Basseterre's cobblestone streets. One of the highlights of my trip was the Brimstone Hill Fortress, a UNESCO World Heritage site. Standing atop it, I admired the magnificent architecture and expansive vistas while picturing the conflicts waged and triumphs achieved there.

St. Kitts and Nevis provided a variety of water-based pleasures in addition to its extensive history. The lure of exploring the colorful underwater environment that lay just beyond the shoreline was too great for me to refuse. I was able to submerge myself in a rainbow of hues when snorkeling and scuba diving off the coast of Nevis, swimming with unique fish and brilliant coral reefs. Experiencing the beauty and variety of aquatic life firsthand was a surreal experience. I felt completely engulfed by the warm Caribbean seas, which left me with a lasting impression of peace and tranquility.

I indulged in the opulent resorts and immaculate beaches of the islands to relax and take in the idyllic surroundings. Azure seas gently kissed the sun-drenched dunes, creating the ideal setting for rest and renewal. Every moment felt like absolute happiness, whether it was eating delicious local food, drinking a tasty cocktail, or just sitting and admiring the captivating sunset.

St. Kitts and Nevis won my heart in ways I never anticipated because to their obvious charm and breathtaking scenery. I went on a journey of self-discovery during which I learned to appreciate the beauty of the world and the simplicity of existence. I will always cherish the memories I made while spending time on these alluring islands since they serve as a constant reminder of the beauty that exists both within and outside of our normal lives.

St. Kitts and Nevis should unquestionably be at the top of your vacation wish list if you're looking for an amazing adventure. Accept the friendly welcome, acquaint yourself with the dynamic culture, and allow the stunning scenery to capture your heart. It's a lifetime journey just waiting to be experienced and imprinted on the fabric of your own recollections.

Welcome to St. Kitts and Nevis

Welcome to St. Kitts and Nevis, two enthralling islands that are a true haven for travelers looking for Caribbean beauty, sun-kissed beaches, and rich cultural experiences. These twin islands, which are located in the eastern Caribbean Sea, are a veritable treasure trove of delights that will take your breath away. So let's travel virtually and find out what wonder St. Kitts and Nevis has in store for you!

The balmy tropical breeze greets you as you exit the plane, and the inhabitants' welcoming grins welcome you right away. In St. Kitts and Nevis, where time seems to stand still and relaxing is a way of life, there is a special blend of Caribbean allure. The islands are well known for their immaculate beaches, where fine white sands meet turquoise waters to provide a picture-perfect landscape. You can find the ideal beach to suit your needs, whether you're looking for a serene area to unwind in or an exciting environment for water sports.

St. Kitts and Nevis provide a window into the past for those who enjoy history and culture. A lengthy and rich history may be found on the islands. Discover Basseterre's lovely alleys lined with colorful structures as you explore the colonial architecture that has been preserved there, which is the capital of St. Kitts. Get there and immerse yourself in the history of the impressive Brimstone Hill Fortress National Recreation Area a member of the UNESCO. The fort's expansive views of the island and the Caribbean Sea provide an incredible vantage point from which to take in the beauty all around you.

You'll come across the friendly, hospitable natives who are proud of their past as you travel the islands. Talk to people in a courteous manner, discover the fascinating traditions, and enjoy the delectable regional cuisine. A delicious blend of African, British, and Caribbean cuisines may be found on St. Kitts and Nevis. Enjoy delectable dishes including spicy stews, fresh seafood, and exotic fruits for a complete culinary trip.

The pristine landscapes and varied ecosystems of St. Kitts and Nevis will fascinate nature lovers. Take a trek through the islands' lush jungles to find secret waterfalls and colorful flora and animals. An old volcano called Mount Liamuiga beckons the intrepid to scale its treacherous slopes and be rewarded with spectacular vistas from its summit. The trekking trails wind through thick vegetation and provide vistas of vibrant birds and amusing monkeys.

But the allure of the islands goes beyond the earth. Divers will discover a colorful underwater environment rich with marine life. Discover coral reefs, go for a swim with exotic fish, or perhaps meet imposing sea turtles. Discovering the hidden treasures beneath the clear seas through snorkeling and diving tours will leave you with priceless memories that you'll cherish long after your trip is finished.

St. Kitts and Nevis provide a variety of activities to suit all interests. Try your luck at the exciting casinos, tee off at top-notch golf courses with stunning ocean vistas, or set out on a catamaran cruise to take in the sun and the calm wind of the Caribbean. There are countless opportunities for excitement and relaxation.

You'll leave St. Kitts and Nevis feeling rejuvenated and with a wealth of treasured memories as the sun sets on your time there. The islands' stunning natural surroundings, friendly people, and rich cultural history come together to make an unforgettable experience. Pack your luggage, embrace your sense of adventure, and get ready to experience the splendor that St. Kitts and Nevis have to offer.

Andrea Townson

CHAPTER ONE

Culture and History

The islands of St. Kitts and Nevis offer a trip through time, allowing you to discover the intriguing stories and heritage that have fashioned these lovely Caribbean gems. The islands are steeped in riveting past and thriving cultural traditions. Let's explore St. Kitts and Nevis's past and present, revealing the many facets of this unique tapestry.

History

The entrance of European explorers, colonialism, and freedom fights are all linked with the history of St. Kitts and Nevis. Before Christopher Columbus discovered the islands in 1493, the native Carib and Arawak peoples lived there. British and French forces fought for possession of the islands, which turned into a battlefield for European powers.

The history of the islands was significantly influenced by the sugar business. Due to its advantageous location and thriving sugar plantations, St. Kitts was referred to as the "Gibraltar of the West Indies" in the 17th and 18th centuries. Forcibly bringing African slaves to the islands to labor on these plantations left a lasting mark on St. Kitts and Nevis' culture and heritage.

The fight for liberation benefited greatly from the contributions made by the islands. The Brimstone Hill Fortress, a UNESCO World Heritage site, is a reminder of the struggles against colonial forces that were fought and won. It stands as a testament to the islanders' tenacity and resolve to retain their independence.

St. Kitts and Nevis has a lively culture that is weaved from many different African, British, and Caribbean influences. The natives sometimes referred to as Kittitians and Nevisians, are extremely proud of their culture and celebrate it via music, dancing, festivals, and food.

An essential component of culture is music. The air is filled with the throbbing rhythms of calypso, reggae, and soca, luring you to sway and dance to their irresistible sounds. The islands have given rise to well-known performers and bands that have permanently impacted the Caribbean music scene.

The most anticipated festival of the year, Carnival, displays the joie de vivre and energy of the Kittitian and Nevisian people. The streets are filled with vibrant costumes, spirited parades, and throbbing music as locals and visitors join forces to joyfully and exuberantly celebrate. It's time to relish in the sense of community and cultural pride while embracing the rhythm of the islands.

The delicious blend of tastes in St. Kitts and Nevis food reflects the unique background of the islands. Delectable recipes that feature recently caught fish, lobster, and conch put seafood center stage. Goat water, a delicious stew, jerk chicken, and other regional specialties delight the palate and offer a distinctive dining experience.

Getting to know the welcoming inhabitants and learning about their traditions and customs is possible when visiting St. Kitts and Nevis. Every interaction evokes a sense of warmth and genuineness, from the age-old crafts of basket weaving and pottery to lively storytelling and folklore. Visitors are warmly welcomed by the Kittitian and Nevisian people, who are ready to share their culture and traditions.

Museums and heritage sites provide a wealth of information for a greater understanding of the history and culture of the islands. The National Museum in Basseterre presents relics, records, and exhibitions that bring the past to life while offering insights into the history of the islands. A visit to the Alexander Hamilton House and the Nevis Heritage Village is especially recommended because they provide insights into the noteworthy inhabitants of the island.

It is a transforming experience to become fully immersed in St. Kitts and Nevis's history and culture. It enables you to recognize the strength of the people, the importance of their heritage, and the vivacious traditions that are still practiced today. You will learn more about the history of the islands as you visit them and come to appreciate the rich tapestry that makes St. Kitts and Nevis so exceptional.

St. Kitts and Nevis Geography

St. Kitts and Nevis, a gorgeous pair of islands in the eastern Caribbean Sea, enchant visitors with their unspoiled beauty and varied topography. Let's travel to St. Kitts and Nevis to learn about its geography, where pristine beaches, lush rainforests, and majestic mountains combine to create a paradise that is visible to all.

The larger of the two islands, St. Kitts, often known as Saint Christopher, is distinguished for its stunning topography. The craggy peaks of Mount Liamuiga, a dormant volcano that soars to a stunning height of 1,156 meters (3,792 ft), dominate the island's central region. The spectacular volcano's slopes are covered in thick rainforests, which act as a sanctuary for a wide range of flora and fauna. The island

and the azure waters surrounding it may be seen in amazing detail from the peak, which is reachable by hiking.

You will find the productive coastal plains that extend along St. Kitts' beaches as you travel past the highlands. These lowlands are home to lush agricultural fields where tropical crops like sugarcane and bananas grow. A gorgeous countryside is created by the lush vegetation and undulating hills, making it ideal for leisurely drives and exploration.

The smaller sister island, Nevis, provides a more serene and private atmosphere. It is renowned for its immaculate beaches, where golden dunes and pure waters meet. With so many hidden coves and bays to explore, Nevis' coastline is a paradise for sunbathers and water sports fans. Nevis has it all, whether you're searching for a tranquil place to unwind or a lively beach for water sports.

Nevis Peak, a dormant volcano that rises to a remarkable height of 985 meters (3,232 feet), dominates the interior of Nevis. Rich rainforests blanket the mountain, providing a haven for a wide variety of plants and fauna. The island is covered in hiking routes that let you discover hidden waterfalls and stunning landscapes while exploring the natural beauties.

The Narrows, a two-mile-wide channel that divides Nevis and St. Kitts, is one of the islands' distinctive characteristics. The nearby island may be seen beautifully from this short strait, which also offers opportunities for sailing, yachting, and other water sports.

The St. Kitts and Nevis islands are fortunate to have a tropical environment with mild temperatures and calming trade winds. A variety of plant and animal species can thrive in the lush greenery and ideal climate provided by the year-round average temperature of roughly 27°C (80°F).

You'll come across a dynamic ecosystem that is home to a variety of creatures as you explore the landscape of St. Kitts and Nevis. The islands are alive with natural delights that are just waiting to be explored, from colorful tropical birds soaring through the skies to lively monkeys swinging through the trees.

The environment of St. Kitts and Nevis provides an incredible backdrop for exploration, adventure, and leisure. The islands will make an everlasting impression on your heart whether you spend time exploring the jungles, relaxing on the beaches, or simply taking in the natural splendor. As you set off on your tour through this Caribbean paradise, get ready to be mesmerized by the natural splendor that unfolds before you.

People of St. Kitts and Nevis

Beyond its beautiful scenery and fascinating history, St. Kitts and Nevis is genuinely brought to life by its friendly and outgoing population. Visitors will have an amazing experience thanks in large part to the genuine warmth and bright spirit of the Kittitians and Nevisians. Let's examine the inhabitants of St. Kitts and Nevis in more detail, as well as the distinctive cultural fabric that they have woven.

The DNA of the Kittitian and Nevisian peoples is one of hospitality. You will be welcomed with open arms and a grin the moment you step foot on the islands. The inhabitants take tremendous pleasure in their community and are happy to introduce tourists to their customs, culture, and natural attractions. You'll encounter a real desire to connect and assist, whether you're looking for advice, ideas, or are just having a simple discussion.

The inhabitants of St. Kitts and Nevis are renowned for having a strong sense of belonging and community. People on the islands take the time to get to know one another and live in a relaxed, friendly environment where everyone knows one another. This sense of harmony is evident at festivals and celebrations where locals and guests mingle to indulge in the jovial spirit of the islands.

St. Kitts and Nevis residents are proud ambassadors of their colorful traditions, and music and dance are deeply ingrained in the island nation's culture. Music and dance play a significant role in daily life, from the pulsating beats of calypso and reggae to the frenetic movements of traditional dances. You'll find yourself tapping your feet and swaying to the contagious rhythms, whether it's a spontaneous street performance or a raucous gathering in a neighborhood pub.

Interacting with the people is a pleasant experience that enables you to learn more about the history, traditions, and way of life of the islands. If you strike up a discussion, you'll be regaled with tales and anecdotes that provide a window into St. Kitts and Nevis's rich cultural history. The inhabitants take pride in conserving and passing down their cultural traditions, which range from folklore and storytelling to traditional crafts like basket weaving and ceramics.

Every culture revolves around food, and the unique traditions of the islands are reflected in the Kittitian and

Nevisian cuisine. To create a distinctive culinary experience, the locals incorporate the tastes and ingredients of African, British, and Caribbean influences. Be ready to indulge in scrumptious meals like jerk chicken, seafood that has just been caught, robust stews, and decadent desserts. Food is an expression of love and hospitality in St. Kitts and Nevis, so don't be shocked if you're invited to attend a community feast or enjoy a handcrafted dish.

The Kittitians and Nevisians take great pride in their own islands, which reflects their strong sense of community. They value their environment, conduct sustainable tourism, and treasure their natural beauty. You'll discover a sincere desire to safeguard the pristine beaches, verdant rainforests, and abundant marine life that make St. Kitts and Nevis a true paradise, as well as the island's distinctive environment.

The warmth, sincerity, and joie de vivre of the Caribbean are personified by St. Kitts & Nevis and its inhabitants. For everyone who visits, the genuine friendliness, lively culture, and strong feeling of community provide an amazing experience. As you establish relationships and make priceless memories with the amazing people of St. Kitts and Nevis, get ready to be embraced by the charm and energy of the islands.

Resources Available in St. Kitts and Nevis

While St. Kitts and Nevis are renowned for their hospitable people and natural beauty, they also have a variety of rich resources that support the sustainability and economic growth of the islands. Let's look at the many resources St. Kitts and Nevis has access to as well as the opportunities they provide.

1. Resources for Agriculture: The fertile soil and tropical climate of the islands provide ideal conditions for agriculture. Sugarcane, bananas, coconuts, and other tropical fruits are grown extensively in St. Kitts and Nevis. The once-dominant sugar business has recently expanded to include other crops, bolstering the economy of the islands and generating employment.

2. Tourism: Because of their stunning natural surroundings, immaculate beaches, and dynamic cultures, St. Kitts and Nevis have long been a favorite travel destination. The tourism sector on the islands contributes significantly to the economy by creating jobs and money. The islands' opulent resorts, exciting festivals, historical monuments, water sports, and eco-tourism opportunities lure tourists, helping the tourism industry to thrive sustainably.

3. Renewable Energy: As part of its dedication to sustainability, St. Kitts and Nevis is embracing renewable energy sources. The islands are perfect for producing solar and wind energy due to their high levels of sunshine and prevailing winds. A greener and more eco-friendly energy sector will result from efforts to utilize these resources and lessen dependency on imported fossil fuels.

4. Marine Resources: St. Kitts and Nevis have access to a variety of marine resources in the nearby Caribbean Sea. Fishing is a significant activity that supports many islanders' livelihoods and provides fresh seafood to the markets and restaurants on the islands. Divers and snorkelers are drawn to the crystal-clear waters, where they may explore the abundant marine life and coral reefs, boosting the ecotourism industry.

5. Financial Services: St. Kitts and Nevis have made a name for themselves as major international hubs for banking, insurance, and investing. The islands have become desirable locations for foreign commerce and investment due to their favorable tax legislation and stable political climate, creating an extra source of income and job possibilities.

6. Human Resources: The people of the islands are the islands' most precious resource. The Kittitian and Nevisian

labor force is renowned for its commitment, competence, and hard work ethic. To provide the local population with the skills needed to prosper in a variety of industries, including tourism, agriculture, finance, and services, education and vocational training programs have been put in place.

In order to promote environmental stewardship and social responsibility, efforts are being undertaken to ensure that the development and exploitation of these resources are sustainable. The government is putting policies and programs into place in conjunction with regional groups and international partners in order to safeguard the natural resources of the islands, maintain their cultural history, and strike a balance between economic growth and environmental preservation.

Rich resources of St. Kitts and Nevis provide a strong foundation for the country's economic development and residents' well-being. The islands are working to build a bright future that strikes a balance between economic success and the preservation of their natural and cultural assets by using these resources wisely and responsibly.

Government

The democratic system of government of St. Kitts and Nevis, a sovereign state in the Caribbean, provides stability, promotes the welfare of its people, and fosters an atmosphere that is conducive to economic growth. Let's examine the St. Kitts and Nevis government's dedication to good governance in more detail.

1. Political Organization: Nevis and St. Kitts is governed by monarchy based on a constitution and practices parliamentary democracy. The British queen, who is now Queen Elizabeth II, is the head of state and is represented by a Governor-General. A prime minister who leads the majority party in the National Assembly serves as the head of state.

2. The legislative body in St. Kitts and Nevis, the National Assembly, is in charge of passing laws and advancing the interests of the populace. It is made up of 14 elected individuals known as Members of Parliament (MPs), 11 of whom represent St. Kitts constituencies and 3 of whom represent Nevis constituencies. Through spirited discussions and the adoption of legislation, the National Assembly makes sure that the voices and concerns of the populace are heard and taken into consideration.

3. Separation of Powers: By maintaining a balance between the executive, legislative, and judicial departments, St. Kitts and Nevis adheres to the concepts of the separation of powers. The Prime Minister serves as the head of the executive branch, which is in charge of overseeing the country's daily administration. The National Assembly is, as was already mentioned, the legislative body. The Supreme Court of the Eastern Caribbean, which represents Nevis and St. Kitts as its final court of appeal, is part of the judicial branch.

4. Human Rights and the Rule of Law: The government of St. Kitts and Nevis supports the fundamental freedoms and rights of its citizens while upholding the principles of the rule of law. The provision of rights in the Constitution—including freedom of expression, assembly, and religion—ensures a democratic and diverse society. The legal system offers a fair and impartial platform for settling conflicts and defending people's rights.

5. Social and Economic Development: The St. Kitts and Nevis administration is dedicated to the nation's social and economic development. Infrastructure development, healthcare, social welfare, and education are all supported through policies and initiatives. The government has put

policies in place to entice investment, diversify the economy, and provide job opportunities for its residents because it understands the value of sustainable economic growth.

St. Kitts and Nevis participates actively in international organizations and preserves diplomatic ties with other nations. The government works to promote trade, cultural exchange, and mutual cooperation while fostering positive relationships and collaborations with the global community.

Good governance, openness, and accountability are highly valued by the government of St. Kitts and Nevis. To secure the welfare and advancement of the country, it interacts with civil society, promotes public engagement, and welcomes comments and constructive criticism.

St. Kitts and Nevis works to establish a setting that fosters social justice, allows for the success of its residents, and sets the path for a prosperous future for future generations through its dedication to democracy, stability, and inclusive administration.

Andrea Townson

CHAPTER TWO

Making Travel Arrangements

Prepare yourself for an extraordinary vacation in the heart of the Caribbean if you're thinking about visiting St. Kitts and Nevis. These twin islands provide a wide range of experiences to enjoy in, from immaculate beaches and lush jungles to rich history and vibrant culture. An itinerary and tips for making the most of your time in this tropical paradise are provided here.

1. Best Time to Visit: St. Kitts and Nevis experiences year-round pleasant weather, with average temperatures of roughly 27°C (80°F). From December through April, when the weather is dry and a little cooler, is considered the busiest travel period. If you want a more tranquil experience, think about going in May to June or November, which are the shoulder seasons. You should check weather forecasts and travel advisories before your journey because the islands are in the storm belt.

2. How to Get There: Robert L. Bradshaw International Airport (SKB), which is on St. Kitts, serves St. Kitts and Nevis. With connections to Europe, North America, and other Caribbean islands, it is serviced by a number of significant airlines. As an alternative, you may fly into one of

the nearby islands, such Antigua or Puerto Rico, and then take a ferry or a subsequent trip to St. Kitts or Nevis.

3. Accommodations: To accommodate every taste and budget, St. Kitts and Nevis each provide a variety of lodging choices. You'll find accommodations to suit your preferences, including guesthouses, boutique hotels, luxury resorts, and vacation rentals. If you want a livelier ambiance with more dining and nightlife options, think about vacationing on St. Kitts, or choose the peace and quiet of Nevis with its quaint plantation inns and isolated beachside resorts.

4. Beaches and Nature Exploration: St. Kitts and Nevis are blessed with beautiful natural surroundings. Take advantage of Nevis's Cockleshell Beach and Pinney's Beach to spend the day relaxing on pristine beaches. Explore the luxuriant jungles and ascend Mount Liamuiga for sweeping vistas. UNESCO World Heritage Site Brimstone Hill Fortress National Park, offers a glimpse into the islands' rich history and breathtaking panoramas, so make sure to pay it a visit.

5. Experience the unique culture of St. Kitts and Nevis by taking part in regional celebrations like the Nevis Culturama Festival or the St. Kitts Music Festival, where you can take in live music, traditional dances, and mouthwatering Caribbean food. Visit historic locations including the Alexander

Hamilton House, where the renowned founding father was born, and Romney Manor, which houses the Caribelle Batik factory.

6. Outdoor Activities: Take part in a variety of outdoor activities to discover the vivid coral reefs abounding with marine life, such as snorkeling or diving. Kayak or take a catamaran ride to find isolated coves and secret bays. Try zip-lining through the rainforest or go on a beautiful stroll to a secret waterfall if you're an adventurer. Golf fans can play on top-notch courses while admiring breathtaking seaside vistas.

7. Enjoy the mouthwatering flavors of Kittitian and Nevisian food, which are the local specialties. Don't forget to sample regional delicacies like jerk chicken, conch fritters, fresh fish, and hearty West Indian stews. To sample the various gastronomic treats that reflect the cultural heritage of the islands, visit neighborhood eateries, seashore shacks, and posh restaurants.

8. St. Kitts and Nevis are typically safe places to visit for tourists, according to safety and travel advice. However, it's always a good idea to observe basic safety precautions, like as protecting your valuables, spending the night in well-lit locations, and abiding by local laws and customs. For

outdoor activities, remember to include sunscreen, insect repellent, and cozy shoes.

Remember to check entrance criteria, such as passport validity and visa needs based on your place of origin, as you prepare for your trip to St. Kitts and Nevis. Having travel insurance that covers medical crises and trip cancellations is also a good idea.

St. Kitts and Nevis provide an unrivaled Caribbean experience with its magnificent scenery, gracious hospitality, and vibrant culture. So gather your belongings, savor the island ambiance, and get ready to make lifelong memories in this lush paradise.

When Should You Visit

1. The dry season—which lasts from December to April—is the ideal time to visit St. Kitts and Nevis. These months often provide bright, pleasant weather with lower humidity levels. This time frame falls during the busiest travel season, so be prepared for larger crowds and increased costs for lodging and entertainment.

2. Consider traveling in May to June or November if you'd want a more sedate experience with fewer tourists. Even

though these months are part of the rainy season, they nevertheless include a lot of bright days, and lodging is frequently available at a discount.

3. The fact that St. Kitts and Nevis are situated within the hurricane belt and that the official hurricane season runs from June to November should not be overlooked. Although the islands have procedures in place to deal with such circumstances, it is advisable to follow weather reports and travel warnings if you intend to visit during this time.

Overall, St. Kitts and Nevis have a comfortable tropical environment year-round, allowing visitors to take advantage of the islands' beauty and attractions whenever they travel there. When choosing the optimum time for your trip, keep in mind your preferences for the weather, the number of tourists, and your budget.

Accessing St. Kitts and Nevis

Travelers have a few options for getting to St. Kitts and Nevis, which makes the process comparatively simple. The principal routes to these stunning Caribbean islands are listed below:

1. By Air: Robert L. Bradshaw International Airport (SKB), which is situated on the island of St. Kitts, serves St. Kitts and Nevis. Major airlines with links to North America, Europe, and other Caribbean locations, including American Airlines, Delta Air Lines, Air Canada, British Airways, and Caribbean Airlines, land at this airport. You can either arrange for a transfer to your accommodation after arriving at SKB or take a quick cab trip there.

2. Flying to a nearby hub, such as San Juan, Puerto Rico, or Antigua, and then catching a connecting flight to Robert L. Bradshaw International Airport, is an option if there are no direct flights from your area to St. Kitts and Nevis. Regular flights between these islands are provided by a number of regional carriers, including LIAT and Winair.

3. Services for Ferries: Another way to get to St. Kitts and Nevis if you're already in the Caribbean is by boarding a ferry. Ferry services are offered from nearby islands like St. Maarten/St. Martin, Antigua, and St. Thomas are American territories. Caribbean islands. A gorgeous and practical method to get to the islands is by ferry, but it's vital to check schedules and availability beforehand.

You can take a quick ferry from Basseterre, the city of St. Kitts, to Charlestown, the capital of Nevis, after you arrive there if your final destination is the sister island of Nevis. The trip takes about 45 minutes and the ferry runs multiple times a day.

To get the best deals and guarantee availability, it's a good idea to purchase your boat or airplane tickets well in advance of your trip, especially during periods of high travel demand.

Regardless of the means of transportation you select, the trip to St. Kitts and Nevis will serve as the starting point for an unforgettable Caribbean vacation brimming with untouched nature, vivacious culture, and friendly people.

How to Navigate St. Kitts and Nevis

Due to their size and sophisticated transportation infrastructure, St. Kitts and Nevis are rather simple to navigate. The primary means of transportation for getting about are listed below:

1. Taxis: On St. Kitts and Nevis, taxis are a practical and well-liked method of transportation. At the ferry docks, airports, and other tourist destinations, taxis are easily accessible. It's a good idea to haggle over the price with the driver before you set off on your trip or make sure the taxi has a meter. For

private trips or all-day excursions to explore the islands, taxis can also be rented.

2. Renting a car is a common choice for tourists who want the flexibility to discover St. Kitts and Nevis at their own speed. Both islands are home to a variety of automobile rental businesses that provide a selection of vehicles to suit various demands and price ranges. Driving is done on the left side of the road, same like in the UK, and a current driver's license is necessary.

3. Public Buses: On St. Kitts and Nevis, public buses, also referred to as "mini-buses," run and offer a reasonably priced mode of transportation. Buses generally serve the local population with predetermined routes and timetables. They can be a wonderful choice for quick excursions within major cities or along well-traveled paths. For thorough island exploration, they might not be as accessible or dependable as taxis or rented cars.

4. Water Taxis: If you're staying on one island and want to visit the other, you can travel between St. Kitts and Nevis using a water taxi. Between Basseterre (St. Kitts) to Charlestown (Nevis), these taxis provide an attractive and practical means of transportation. Schedules are normally

available at the ferry stations, and the trip takes around 45 minutes.

5. Walking and bicycling: St. Kitts and Nevis have stunning scenery, and certain regions are simple to navigate on foot. The towns, beaches, and historical monuments may all be explored on foot while taking in the surrounding natural splendor. Renting a bicycle also gives you the opportunity to take leisurely rides through quaint villages or along gorgeous seaside routes.

Consider the nature of your activities, the distance you need to go, and your preferences for ease and flexibility as you arrange your transportation alternatives. When evaluating trip times, don't forget to take into account regional traffic conditions and peak travel hours.

Getting around St. Kitts and Nevis is part of the journey, and whichever method of transportation you use, you'll have the chance to learn about the gorgeous landscapes, welcoming towns, and vibrant culture of the islands.

The Best Places to Stay in St. Kitts and Nevis

A crucial step in arranging your vacation to St. Kitts and Nevis is picking the correct lodging. The Islands offer a variety of lodging options. to suit all budgets and interests, whether you're seeking for opulent resorts, stylish boutique hotels, or lovely guesthouses. When choosing your accommodations, keep the following in mind:

1. Place: Think about where in St. Kitts and Nevis you want to stay. The bigger and more developed island is St. Kitts, which has thriving cities, more dining and entertainment options, and more activities and attractions. Nevis, on the other hand, boasts stunning beaches, historic monuments, and a calm ambience in addition to a quieter and more relaxed vibe. Select a place to stay that will give you the experience you want.

2. Accommodation Types: St. Kitts and Nevis offers a selection of lodging options, including five-star resorts, all-inclusive hotels, boutique hotels, bed and breakfasts, and vacation rentals. Consider your ideal housing style and the features that are most essential to you. Restaurants, swimming pools, spas, and recreational activities are just a few of the many amenities that resorts frequently offer. While boutique hotels offer a certain charm and character, guesthouses and vacation rentals provide a more individualized and intimate experience.

3. Budget: Establish a spending limit for your lodging and hunt for possibilities that fall within it. Remember that costs can change depending on the area, the time of year, and the amount of luxury. Due to its smaller size and more upscale resorts, Nevis may cost a little more to stay in than St. Kitts. To get the best rates, look for discounts and other special offers and think about making reservations in advance.

4. Facilities and Amenities: Take into account the facilities and amenities that are significant to you. You might prefer a hotel with a pool or family-friendly activities if you're traveling with children. If you like to play golf or go to the spa, check for hotels that have these features. Look into nearby or on-site dining alternatives, Wi-Fi accessibility, parking options, and any other special needs you may have.

5. Evaluations and Recommendations: To obtain a sense of the level of quality and service offered by various lodgings, read evaluations from prior visitors. Websites like Booking.com and TripAdvisor might be useful for getting opinions and advice from other travelers. Take into account suggestions from friends, online travel communities, or regional authorities who may have first-hand knowledge of the top accommodations.

St. Kitts and Nevis provide a variety of distinctive lodging opportunities. You have the option of staying in beachside cottages, eco-friendly resorts, or restored plantation homes. These choices give you a strong sense of location and let you fully experience the surroundings and culture of the area.

The best lodging option ultimately relies on your particular tastes, financial situation, and the kind of experience you're looking for. The beauty of St. Kitts and Nevis will surround you whether you choose luxury or simplicity, a resort or a guesthouse, and the warm welcome of the inhabitants will make your stay memorable.

What to Bring

It's important to take the tropical temperature and the activities you intend to participate in into account while preparing for your trip to St. Kitts and Nevis. To assist you in getting ready for your vacation, here is a packing list:

1. Pack breathable, light-weight clothing that is appropriate for warm temperatures. To stay cool, use loose-fitting clothing made of natural materials like cotton or linen. Include light-weight slacks or skirts, T-shirts, sundresses,

and shorts. Don't forget your swimsuit so you can enjoy the gorgeous beaches and pools.

2. Sun protection: Because St. Kitts and Nevis receive a lot of sunshine; bring the necessary sun protection gear. Bring a wide-brimmed hat, UV-protective sunglasses, and high SPF sunscreen. For additional protection while swimming or participating in water sports, think about wearing a rash guard or a thin cover-up.

3. Mosquito repellent: Particularly around dawn and dusk, mosquitoes can be a problem in some regions. To prevent bites, include insect repellent containing DEET or other powerful chemicals.

4. Pack comfortable shoes that are appropriate for walking and other outdoor activities. Ideal footwear includes flip-flops, sandals, and light running or walking shoes. Consider wearing sturdy hiking shoes or sneakers if you intend to hike or explore nature trails.

5. Light layers: Especially in the winter, evenings can be a little bit chilly. For cooler evenings or places with air conditioning, including restaurants and shopping centers, bring a lightweight jacket or sweater.

6. Wear rain gear: St. Kitts and Nevis occasionally suffer showers of rain, particularly during the rainy season. Carry a small, lightweight raincoat or umbrella to protect yourself from unforeseen downpours.

7. Beach essentials: Remember to bring along everything you'll need for the beach, including a beach towel, beach bag, and a foldable beach umbrella or sunshade. If you intend to explore underwater, snorkeling equipment, water shoes, and a waterproof backpack or pouch for valuables are also helpful.

8. Travel adapters: St. Kitts and Nevis use 230V electrical outlets, so if your electronics need a different voltage or plug type, think about packing a travel adapter.

9. First aid kit and drugs: If you regularly use prescription medications, make sure you have enough on hand for the duration of your trip. Pack a basic first aid kit with all the necessary over-the-counter drugs, sticky bandages, and painkillers and antihistamines.

10. Travel documents: Don't forget to pack your passport, details for your travel insurance, and any required visas or permits. Keep these records in a place that is both safe and convenient.

Other things to pack: You should also think about bringing a reusable water bottle, a daypack or beach bag, a camera or smart phone for taking pictures, and any additional personal goods or toiletries you might require.

Keep in mind to travel light and just bring what you really need to. If necessary, the majority of things are readily available on the islands. You'll be ready to take advantage of St. Kitts and Nevis's beauty and adventures if you pack the necessary items in your luggage.

Entry Requirements and Visas

Depending on your nation of citizenship, St. Kitts and Nevis has different visa and entry procedures. Here are some broad recommendations, however it's crucial to confirm the particular needs based on your nationality:

1. Visa Exemptions: If their stay in St. Kitts and Nevis is for shorter than a predetermined amount of time, citizens of a few countries are not required to have a visa. For instance, admission without a visa is frequently permitted for up to 90 days for nationals of the United States, Canada, the United Kingdom, and many other European Union nations. To find out if you are eligible for visa exemptions, see the

government of St. Kitts and Nevis' official website or get in touch with the closest embassy or consulate.

2. Validity of Passport: Ensure your passport remains active for at least six months after the day you intend to exit St. Kitts and Nevis. Check the precise requirements since some nations may want a longer validity time. If you are not entitled to entry without a visa, you may need to apply for a visa in advance. To learn more about the procedure for applying for a visa, the paperwork needed, and the turnaround dates, get in touch with the St. Kitts and Nevis embassy or consulate that is closest to you. Applying for a visa is best done well in advance of your intended travel dates.

3. Return or Onward Ticket: St. Kitts and Nevis immigration authorities may impose a requirement for admission that includes presenting documentation of a return or onward ticket. Make sure you have a certified itinerary showing that you intend to leave the country within the permitted time.

4. Yellow Fever Vaccination: You can be asked to show a certificate of yellow fever vaccination upon arrival if you are traveling to or from a country where there is a risk of yellow fever transmission. Check your travel history to see if this

requirement applies to you, then speak with your doctor about the recommended vaccinations.

Entrance criteria are subject to change, so it's always a good idea to double-check the most recent details before your trip. For the most recent information on visa and entry requirements, consult the government of St. Kitts and Nevis' official website or get in touch with their embassy or consulate.

Before leaving for St. Kitts and Nevis, make sure you have sufficient travel insurance that covers unexpected situations like medical problems and trip cancellation.

Financial and Exchange

The Eastern Caribbean dollar (XCD) is St. Kitts and Nevis' national currency. What you should know about money and exchange in St. Kitts and Nevis is as follows:

1. Eastern Caribbean Dollar: The official money of St. Kitts and Nevis is the Eastern Caribbean dollar. It is also utilized in a number of other Caribbean nations, such as Dominica, Grenada, St. Lucia, Antigua and Barbuda, and St. Vincent

and the Grenadines. The unit of money is the cent, and it is represented by the symbol "$" or "EC$".

2. Exchange Rates: The Eastern Caribbean dollar is pegged at 2.70 EC dollars to 1 USD, with the United States dollar (USD) serving as the reserve currency. This indicates that the Eastern Caribbean dollar's exchange rate with the US dollar is largely constant. Before exchanging money, it's a good idea to verify the current rates because exchange rates can vary somewhat.

3. Currency Exchange: St. Kitts' International Airport Robert L. Bradshaw offers currency exchange services, as do banks and authorized foreign exchange offices in significant cities and popular tourist destinations. Major credit cards like Visa, MasterCard, and American Express are often accepted, but it's still a good idea to have extra cash on hand for local shops, markets, and transportation.

4. Automated Teller Machines (ATMs): St. Kitts and Nevis has a sizable number of ATMs. They can frequently be found in banks, retail malls, and tourist destinations. While most ATMs only dispense Eastern Caribbean currencies, some can also let you withdraw US money. For information on potential overseas transaction fees or withdrawal caps, check with your bank or Credit Card Company.

U.S. U.S. dollars are accepted almost everywhere in St. Kitts and Nevis, particularly in the tourist regions. You might get your change in Eastern Caribbean dollars, though. The ease of carrying lower US dollar denominations is advised.

5. Currency Exchange Advice: It's advised to exchange a small sum of cash upon arrival to cover any immediate expenses like travel or food. To make sure you're getting a fair rate on greater amounts, compare conversion rates and fees with banks and exchange bureaus. In order to avoid any problems using your cards abroad, you should also let your bank or card issuer know about your vacation intentions.

6. Traveler's checks: In St. Kitts and Nevis, they are typically not readily recognized. For transactions, cash or credit/debit cards are more practical.

While traveling, bear in mind to secure your belongings and cash. For flexibility, it's a good idea to have a variety of payment methods on hand, such as cash and credit cards.

Speaking and Interaction

English is Nevis' and St. Kitts official language, making communication for English-speaking tourists to the island very simple. In St. Kitts and Nevis, language and communication are important because of the following reasons:

1. English is a commonly used and understood language on all of the islands. You won't have any issues interacting with locals, hotel and resort employees, and in the majority of tourist sites. Although the regional accent and dialect may differ significantly, English speakers shouldn't encounter any major difficulties.

2. Despite the fact that English is the dominant language, you might encounter some regional slang exclusive to St. Kitts and Nevis. Having conversations with locals might give you the chance to understand and appreciate the subtleties of their language. If you come across any terminology or expressions that are unclear, don't be afraid to ask for clarification.

3. Staff workers that speak many languages are common in the tourism sector, especially at hotels, resorts, and well-known tourist destinations. They may also speak Spanish, French, or German, which is advantageous for visitors from other countries.

4. Communication in Rural regions: You might discover fewer English speakers in more rural or distant regions,

particularly on the island of Nevis. Basic conversation should still be possible, though, and people are typically hospitable and understanding.

5. Mobile networks and the Internet are both well-developed in St. Kitts and Nevis, and coverage is generally dependable. For communication, you can buy local SIM cards or turn on international roaming on your mobile device. Additionally, a lot of hotels, eateries, and coffee shops provide free Wi-Fi so you can stay connected.

6. Emergency Services: To contact the neighborhood's emergency services, such as the police, ambulance, or fire department, phone 911 in the event of an emergency. It's a good idea to keep the embassy or consulate of your country's contact information close to hand in case you need assistance.

Despite the fact that English is widely spoken, it's crucial to be sensitive to cultural norms and distinctions. Positive encounters with locals can be facilitated by being kind, respectful, and friendly.

Keep in mind that language is an effective means of interaction and cultural exchange. A smile and an openness to learning and understanding can overcome language difficulties and help you forge deep connections with St. Kitts and Nevis residents.

Budget Proposed

The recommended spending limit for a trip to St. Kitts and Nevis may change depending on your travel preferences, lodging selections, food tastes, and scheduled activities. Here is an overview of costs to assist you in creating your budget:

1. Accommodations: St. Kitts and Nevis offers a variety of lodging options, from inexpensive guesthouses and vacation rentals to opulent resorts. For mid-range lodging, you should budget between $100 to $300 per night on average. Luxury hotels might charge more than $500 per night.

2. Meals: St. Kitts and Nevis offers a variety of dining alternatives, from casual joints to fine dining establishments. Depending on where and what you decide to eat, meal costs can also change. A three-course lunch at a midrange restaurant may run between $30 and $50 per person, whereas a simple meal at a neighborhood restaurant or street seller may cost between $10 and $20. A lunch at a fine dining restaurant could cost $50 or more.

3. Buses and taxis make up the majority of St. Kitts and Nevis' public transit system. The cost of a bus ride often ranges from $1 to $3. The cost of a taxi varies according on the distance and is negotiated. Another choice is to rent a car, with daily rates starting at $40 to $60.

4. Beach activities, snorkeling, boat tours, hiking, and historical site visits are just a few of the activities and excursions that St. Kitts and Nevis has to offer. Depending on the service and the provider, prices change. While admission fees to sights might cost anywhere from $5 to $20, guided tours can cost anywhere from $50 to $150 per person.

5. Other Expenses: Additional personal costs, travel insurance, visa fees (if necessary), souvenirs, drinks, and other sundries should all be taken into account. You should set aside money in your budget for unforeseen costs and personal preferences.

Overall, $150 to $250 a day, per person, would be a reasonable budget for a comfortable trip to St. Kitts and Nevis. This budget includes some activities or excursions, some public transportation, and midrange lodging, dining, and transportation. It also includes some local and midrange restaurants for eating. Depending on your preferences and the activities you have planned, adjust your budget accordingly.

To construct a thorough budget that meets your trip style and tastes, don't forget to account for any additional expenses, such as international flights, travel insurance, specialized activities, or upscale hotels.

Savings Advice

1. Consider traveling during the off-peak season, which is normally between May and November, when hotel and flight costs are likely to be lower. During this time, you can frequently get better offers and discounts.

2. Explore a variety of lodging choices to see which one offers the best value for your money. In comparison to huge resorts, take into account guesthouses, vacation rentals, or smaller boutique hotels.

3. Self-Catering: Choose hotels with kitchen amenities to reduce meal costs. This enables you to cook some of your meals with items from local markets or grocery stores. It's an excellent way to taste regional cuisine on a budget.

4. Local Restaurants: Check out neighborhood restaurants and street food stands for delectable and reasonably priced fare. Authentic food is frequently available at these places for less money than at posh dining locations.

5. Public transportation: To go about the islands, take the regional bus system. Buses are typically affordable and an excellent way to get a feel for the community. As an alternative, think about splitting the cost of taxis or carpooling with other travelers.

6. Activities that are Free or Very Cheap: St. Kitts and Nevis provide stunning beaches, hiking trails, and historical sites that can be explored for Free or Very Cheap. Visit public parks, take use of the free or inexpensive activities available, and take in the natural beauty of the islands by swimming, snorkeling, and picnicking.

7. Research and Preparation: Do your homework and make a plan before you start. Look for special offers, bundles, and discounts on excursions and activities. For any ongoing deals or limited-time discounts, search regional travel forums, social media pages, and local tourism websites.

8. Water Activities: Instead than paying for pricey guided snorkeling tours, bring your own equipment or rent it from

nearby stores. Numerous St. Kitts and Nevis beaches provide excellent snorkeling opportunities straight off the shore.

8. Avoid the busiest tourist areas and instead explore St. Kitts & Nevis' less-frequented locales. Compared to popular tourist destinations, these locales frequently offer lower costs for food, shopping, and lodging.

9. Tap water is available in St. Kitts and Nevis, so stay hydrated there. Carry a reusable water bottle and fill it with tap water to save money and prevent plastic waste instead of buying bottled water.

Never forget that giving up experiences to save money. You may have a memorable trip to St. Kitts and Nevis while staying within your spending limit by practicing financial restraint, investigating available options locally, and making advance plans.

Top Travel Booking Sites

There are a number of well-known websites and tools that you may use to compare prices and possibilities when making your travel arrangements to St. Kitts and Nevis. Here are some recommended travel agencies:

1. Online travel agencies (OTAs): Sites like Expedia, Booking.com, and Travelocity provide a variety of choices for trips, lodging, and flights. You can easily compare costs, read reviews, and make bookings using these services.

2. Visit the official tourism websites of St. Kitts and Nevis for details on lodging options, points of interest, and travel advice. These websites frequently offer direct booking links to reliable local tour operators and lodgings, enabling you to do so.

3. Websites of hotels and resorts: If you have a certain hotel or resort in mind, it's worthwhile to check their official websites for special offers, discounts, and packages. When making a direct reservation through their websites, several resorts give customers exclusive discounts and extra bonuses.

4. Websites for Vacation Rentals: A variety of vacation rentals, including apartments, homes, and villas, are available on websites like Airbnb, HomeAway, and VRBO. These sites frequently offer a variety of lodging choices at different pricing points, giving you more possibilities.

5. Travel Companies: Speak with companies that specialize in Caribbean vacations. They may provide you with individualized support in organizing your trip, including

booking flights, lodging, travel, and activities. Travel agents could have access to special offers and industry insider information.

6. Online deal aggregators: Sites like Kayak and Skyscanner compile offers from numerous sources, making it possible for you to compare costs and choose the finest flights, lodgings, and vehicle rentals. They can assist you in locating the travel options that are the most affordable.

7. Loyalty Programs and Memberships: If you belong to an airline or hotel loyalty program, think about using your points or incentives to make your travel arrangements. This could result in you paying less for travel and lodging or perhaps getting more benefits and upgrades.

8. Local Tour Operators: Take into account making direct reservations with regional tour operators for St. Kitts and Nevis excursions, tours, and activities. They frequently help the neighborhood economy while offering a more individualized and comprehensive experience. To make sure you select trusted operators, do your homework and check reviews.

Before making any reservations, keep in mind to compare prices, read reviews, and review cancellation conditions. To get the greatest rates and availability, it's also a good idea to book far in advance, especially during busy travel times.

Andrea Townson

CHAPTER THREE

Exploring St. Kitts

The natural splendor, historical sites, and cultural experiences in St. Kitts are many. To make the most of your time on the island, consider participating in the following attractions and activities:

1. The UNESCO World Heritage Site Brimstone Hill stronghold National Park is a magnificent stronghold built on a mountaintop with sweeping views of the island and the Caribbean Sea. Visit the museum, take a tour of the defenses, and discover the history of the island.

2. Basseterre, the nation's capital, is a lively center with colonial buildings, active marketplaces, and important historical sites. Wander around the lively alleys lined with independent stores and coffee shops, stop by the Berkeley Memorial Clock, and meander along Independence Square.

3. Romney Manor & Caribelle Batik: The Caribelle Batik studio and a beautifully kept estate are both located in Old Road Village's Romney Manor. Explore the serene surroundings, see the colorful artwork, and learn about the traditional batik printing technique.

4. Mount Liamuiga: The tallest peak in St. Kitts, Mount Liamuiga, is a must-climb for intrepid hikers. The trek is difficult but rewarding, passing through lava formations and jungles, and the summit gives stunning vistas.

5. St. Kitts is endowed with beautiful beaches. Frigate Bay, South Friars Bay, Cockleshell Bay, and Dieppe Bay are a few of the well-known ones. Spend days lying about on golden beaches, swimming in pristine waters, and engaging in water hobbies such as stand-up kayaking and snorkeling.

6. Explore the beautiful rainforest and natural parks on the island, including the Central Forest Reserve and the Wingfield River Valley. Explore St. Kitts' unique flora and fauna by going on guided walks or zipping through the forest canopy.

7. St. Kitts Scenic Railway: Take a memorable trip on the 30-mile narrow-gauge railway that circles the island of St. Kitts, often known as the "Sugar Train." From here, you'll get breathtaking views of the island's coastline, interior, and sugar cane fields.

8. Cultural Experiences: Participate in local festivals like the St. Kitts Music Festival or the Carnival celebrations to fully immerse yourself in the community's culture. Learn about the island's history, sample regional food, and take in live

music performances at seaside taverns and restaurants by visiting the National Museum.

9. Snorkeling and Catamaran Cruises: Take a catamaran cruise or boat tour of the island, which frequently makes stops for these activities. The seas are usually clear and inviting. Discover coral reefs, interact with abundant marine life, and spend a relaxing and exciting day at sea.

Visit eco-parks and gardens, such as the Romney Gardens and Botanical Garden, to take in the diverse array of tropical flora and flowers as well as the island's incredibly rich biodiversity.

Keep in mind to check the hours of operation, reserve guided tours in advance if necessary, and exercise caution to preserve the environment and observe regional laws and customs. You'll have enduring recollections of St. Kitts' breathtaking natural beauty, engrossing history, and gracious Caribbean hospitality after seeing the island.

City of the Capital: Basseterre

The dynamic and picturesque capital of St. Kitts and Nevis, Basseterre, is home to a variety of colonial history, cultural experiences, and contemporary attractions. What you can discover at Basseterre is as follows:

1. Independence Square: Independence Square, a popular gathering spot and historic monument, is a great place to start your stay in the center of Basseterre. Admire the stunning Georgian-style structures, such as the Old Treasury Building and St. George's Anglican Church. Numerous events and festivals are held in this area.

2. The Circus is a key roundabout and a well-liked gathering spot in Basseterre. It was designed after London's Piccadilly Circus. There are shops, eateries, and cafes all around it. Take a leisurely stroll, take in the bustling environment, and people-watch.

3. The National Museum is housed in the Old Secretariat Palace, which offers information on the history and culture of St. Kitts and Nevis. Learn more about the island's colonial past, indigenous heritage, sugar industry, and struggle for freedom by visiting the exhibitions.

4. The Berkeley Memorial Clock is a well-known monument in Basseterre and is located in Independence Square. Thomas Berkeley Hardtman Berkeley, a previous leader of the Federal Assembly, was honored by having it built.

5. Visit the historic St. George's Anglican Church, an important site for both religious and architectural reasons. This Anglican church, which was built in the 17th century, has serene surroundings and lovely stained glass windows.

6. Port Zante: As St. Kitts' primary cruise ship port, Port Zante is a thriving neighborhood with duty-free stores, boutiques, restaurants, and entertainment options. Shopping for trinkets, jewelry, and handcrafted goods is fun. You may also unwind with a drink at one of the waterfront bars.

7. Craft Market: The Craft Market is a bustling location close to the cruise ship terminal where regional artists sell their original works of art, handmade crafts, apparel, and mementos. Look around the stalls to locate one-of-a-kind souvenirs of your trip and to support regional artisans.

8. Fairview Great House and Botanical Garden: The Hillside Great Hall and Botanical Garden located not far from Basseterre. Tours of this 18th-century mansion are available on a guided basis, plantation house are available, and they include a stroll around the lovely gardens and information on the history of the island.

9. If you enjoy sports, you might want to attend a cricket or football game at Warner Park Sporting Complex. All year

long, a variety of sporting competitions and activities are held at this multipurpose athletic facility.

10. Local Cuisine: Indulge in St. Kitts delicacies at the neighborhood diners and restaurants in Basseterre. Consider traditional fare like conch fritters, goat water, and stewed salt fish. Don't forget to try some of the island's favorite beverage, local rum.

Basseterre is a wonderful area to visit and take in the culture of the island because of its fascinating history, endearing architecture, and lively environment. Take your time to explore the city's streets, mingle with the populace, and uncover its own charm.

Square Independence

In the center of Basseterre, the capital of St. Kitts and Nevis, you'll find Independence Square, a scenic and historically significant square. It is significant historically and culturally, and it is a thriving meeting spot for both locals and tourists. What to expect in Independence Square is as follows:

1. Independence Square is a symbolic location with significant historical significance for St. Kitts and Nevis. Pall Mall Square was its previous name during British colonial

administration; it was renamed in 1983 to celebrate the country's independence from British domination.

2. Independence Square is conveniently located in the heart of Basseterre and acts as the hub for many different events and activities. It is surrounded by significant landmarks, governmental structures, retail establishments, and eateries, making it a busy and lively area of the city.

3. Berkeley Memorial Clock: The Berkeley Memorial Clock is a prominent element of Independence Square. In 1883, Thomas Berkeley Hardtman Berkeley, former head of the Supreme Legislative Board, had this elaborate clock tower built in his honor. A well-known landmark and gathering place for both locals and visitors is the clock tower.

4. Georgian-style architecture: The square is bordered by lovely structures in the Georgian style, which adds to its allure and vintage feel. These structures have brightly colored facades and colonial-era architectural accents.

5. Open-Air Location: Independence Square is a well-liked location for a variety of cultural events, festivals, and meetings all year round. The square hosts concerts, plays, parades, and Independence Day celebrations that highlight the unique culture and customs of St. Kitts and Nevis.

6. St. George's Anglican Church is a historic building that is situated close to Independence Square. This lovely church, which was built in the early 19th century, has beautiful stained glass windows and intricate architectural features. It is a noteworthy religious and historical site that is worth seeing.

7. Local markets and sellers may be found all around Independence Square selling a range of products, including fresh food, regional crafts, mementos, and artwork. The local culture can be fully experienced while you shop for unusual things there.

Independence Square provides a calm and friendly atmosphere where you may take a rest, sit on a bench, and take in the busy city life. It's a great place to people-watch, take in some Caribbean rays, and take in Basseterre's atmosphere.

Independence Square is a prominent and energetic location that captures the spirit of St. Kitts and Nevis, whether you are there to take in the ambiance, take in an exciting event, or learn about the history of the island.

National Gallery

In Basseterre, the capital of St. Kitts, there is a cultural establishment called the National Museum of St. Kitts and Nevis. It is committed to safeguarding and showcasing the island nation's unique history, culture, and heritage. A fascinating look into the history and a better understanding of the island's identity are provided by a visit to the National Museum. What to look for at the National Museum is listed below:

1. Historical Displays: The museum offers a variety of historical displays from various eras in St. Kitts and Nevis history. The displays shed light on the island's past, covering everything from the native Amerindian people to the colonial era and the struggle for independence. You can investigate relics, records, pictures, and interactive exhibits that illuminate various facets of the history of the country.

2. Colonial Era: Learn about the island's colonial history and its involvement in the sugar business, which was important to the economy of St. Kitts and Nevis. Discover the island's influence of European colonization, including the arrival of several European powers and the legacy they left behind.

3. Amerindian Heritage: The museum celebrates the indigenous Amerindian people that previously inhabited the

islands. Explore exhibits that showcase their way of life, artifacts, and role in the island's early history.

4. Folklore and Traditions: Learn about St. Kitts and Nevis's distinct folklore, traditions, and customs. Exhibits featuring traditional music, dancing, storytelling, and the vivid Carnival celebrations that take place on the islands are frequently included at the museum.

5. Natural History: Discover St. Kitts and Nevis' various ecosystems, plants, and animals. The museum highlights the island's natural beauty and biodiversity, including information on marine life, rainforests, and rare animals.

6. Cultural items: The National Museum houses a collection of cultural items such as tools, clothing, ceramics, and artwork that depict the island's cultural legacy. These exhibits offer an insight into the daily lives and artistic expressions of St. Kitts and Nevis residents.

7. Educational Programs: For visitors of all ages, the museum frequently conducts educational programs, workshops, and events. These initiatives seek to raise public awareness and appreciation of the nation's history and cultural heritage.

8. Gift store: Before leaving the museum, stop by the gift store to find one-of-a-kind souvenirs, locally manufactured crafts, books, and artwork that reflect St. Kitts and Nevis' culture and heritage.

A trip to the National Museum is a gratifying experience for history aficionados, cultural enthusiasts, and everyone interested in learning about St. Kitts and Nevis' diverse heritage. It gives a detailed history of the island and its significance in establishing the nation's identity.

National Park of Brimstone Hill Fortress

Brimstone Hill Fortress National Park is a UNESCO World Heritage Site and one of St. Kitts and Nevis' most recognizable and historically significant attractions. The stronghold, perched atop a high hill on St. Kitts' western shore, provides stunning panoramic views of the surrounding landscapes and the Caribbean Sea. Here's what to expect when you go to Brimstone Hill Fortress:

1. Brimstone Hill Fortress is a testimony to the island's rich history and strategic significance. The fortress, built between the 17th and 18th centuries, operated as a military stronghold and played an important role in protecting the

island from invasions and raids. It represents the island's endurance and strategic importance throughout colonial times.

2. Architectural Wonder: The stronghold is well-known for its outstanding architectural design and engineering. The masonry and defenses were painstakingly constructed from locally available volcanic rock, resulting in a visually magnificent and formidable building. Explore the well-preserved walls, bastions, and defensive structures and marvel at past artistry.

3. Fort George Citadel: The Fort George Citadel is the fortress's showpiece, an enormous building with breathtaking views of the surrounding surroundings. Explore the interior of the citadel, which houses a museum with artifacts, displays, and multimedia presentations about the fortress's history and significance.

4. Panoramic Views: From the summit of Brimstone Hill, you'll have panoramic views of the Caribbean Sea, surrounding islands, and St. Kitts' beautiful green landscapes. Take your time admiring the breathtaking scenery and snapping photos.

5. Museum and Interpretive Center: The park has a museum and interpretive center that provide additional information

about the fortress's history and cultural significance. Learn about colonialism's influence, the daily lives of soldiers stationed at Brimstone Hill, and the role Brimstone Hill played in regional battles.

6. Nature & Wildlife: Brimstone Hill Fortress National Park is a sanctuary for biodiversity as well as a historical landmark. The park is home to a variety of bird species as well as lush greenery and tropical plants. As you explore the grounds, keep a look out for indigenous flora and fauna.

7. Guided Tours: Attending a Brimstone Hill Fortress guided tour is highly recommended. Knowledgeable guides can provide extensive information, anecdotes, and historical context to help you better understand and appreciate the site. Access to sites not open to the general public may also be included in guided tours.

8. Visitor Facilities: The park contains visitor facilities, such as a gift shop where you may buy souvenirs and booklets about the stronghold and the history of the island. There is also a café where you may sip refreshments while admiring the breathtaking scenery.

Brimstone Hill Fortress National Park is a remarkable excursion into the island's past, combining history, breathtaking architecture, natural beauty, and expansive views. It is a must-see location for history buffs, architecture lovers, and anybody interested in learning more about St. Kitts and Nevis' rich heritage.

Romney House

Romney Manor, also known as Caribelle Batik at Romney Manor, is a St. Kitts historic landmark and botanical garden. It provides a one-of-a-kind combination of natural beauty, cultural legacy, and artistic expression. Here's what to expect when you visit Romney Manor:

1. Romney Manor has a long history dating back to the 17th century. A British colonial family originally had a sugarcane plantation here. Today, the manor serves as a museum of the island's history, giving tourists a glimpse into the colonial era and the plantation's importance in the island's history.

2. Romney Manor's grounds include a stunning botanical garden filled with lush tropical flora, colorful flowers, and towering trees. Take a stroll in the garden and take in the peace and natural beauty that surrounds you. Take in the range of plant species, including exotic orchids and vibrant blossoms.

3. Romney Manor is well-known for being the home of Caribelle Batik, a renowned batik studio and shop. Batik is a classic textile art form in which fabric is hand-dyed using wax-resist processes. Visit the workshop to see the experienced artists make beautiful designs on fabric, or buy for one-of-a-kind batik clothes, accessories, and home décor products.

4. The magnificent ancient Saman tree is one of the centerpieces of Romney Manor. This enormous tree is thought to be around 350 years old and is one of the Caribbean's largest of its kind. The tree's sprawling branches and massive size provide a shady refuge and an ideal location for rest and photography.

5. Cultural Demonstrations: At Romney Manor, visitors can see cultural demonstrations that display traditional St. Kitts crafts and activities. Learn about local traditions and immerse yourself in the island's cultural history by watching artists manufacture handmade crafts.

6. Picnic sites: If you're searching for a pleasant location to relax and enjoy a picnic surrounded by nature, Romney Manor has picnic sites where you can unwind and enjoy the tranquil ambiance of the botanical gardens.

7. Romney Manor's gift shop and café provide unique souvenirs, batik products, local artwork, and other Caribbean-inspired items. There is also a café serving refreshments, light snacks, and local delicacies.

8. Events and Workshops: Romney Manor presents a variety of events, workshops, and cultural activities throughout the year. Check the schedule for any special events taking place during your visit, since these can provide additional insights into the island's traditions and cultural heritage.

Romney Manor combines natural beauty, artistic expression, and cultural history in a pleasant way. It is a must-see site for people looking for a quiet and engaging experience that embraces St. Kitts' particular beauty.

Batik Caribelle

Caribelle Batik is a well-known batik studio and shop in Romney Manor, St. Kitts. It is a popular attraction for travelers who want to see how exquisite batik designs are created and buy unique batik apparel, accessories, and home décor products. Here's what to expect when you visit Caribelle Batik:

1. Caribelle Batik is well-known for its traditional batik production process. Batik is a method of creating elaborate and colorful motifs by putting wax to fabric and then coloring it. At the workshop, you can watch expert artists at work, using hot wax and various tools to create stunning patterns on fabric.

2. Witnessing the batik-making process at Caribelle Batik is an enthralling experience. You can witness firsthand how the artisans delicately construct elaborate designs using a combination of wax and brilliant colors, from the initial wax application to the delicate dyeing process.

3. Caribelle Batik offers a wide choice of distinctive designs, each showcasing the craftsmen' creativity and craftsmanship. The designs range from traditional Caribbean motifs to modern patterns, so there is something for everyone's taste and flair.

4. Handmade items: Caribelle Batik's items are all handcrafted with care and precision. From clothes like skirts, blouses, and sarongs to accessories like scarves, bags, and ties, there's a wide range of batik things to choose from. These handcrafted items make for one-of-a-kind and memorable mementos or gifts.

5. Caribelle Batik also offers custom orders if you have a certain design in mind. You can talk to the craftspeople about your ideas and preferences, and they will work with you to create a one-of-a-kind batik creation that is suited to your specifications.

6. Shopping Experience: Caribelle Batik's shop offers a great shopping experience. Take your time looking through the attractively arranged products and finding the right batik piece to take home. The courteous and experienced team is always ready to help and share their expertise of the art of batik.

7. Caribelle Batik periodically hosts batik classes where guests can learn the fundamentals of batik-making and create their own unique designs. These workshops offer hands-on experience and a greater understanding of the art form.

8. Cultural Immersion: A visit to Caribelle Batik not only allows you to view the artistic creations but also provides insight into St. Kitts' cultural history. Batik designs are frequently inspired by the island's natural beauty, folklore, and traditions, offering a link to the local culture.

Caribelle Batik at Romney Manor is a must-see for art aficionados, fashionistas, and anyone interested in the creative process of batik-making. It provides the opportunity of a lifetime to observe the beauty of batik manufacturing, buy high-quality handcrafted products, and bring a piece of Caribbean craftsmanship home with you.

Bay of Frigates

Frigate Bay is a scenic coastal spot on St. Kitts' southern shore. It is a popular tourist and local attraction, noted for its stunning beaches, active nightlife, and diverse recreational opportunities. Here's what to expect when you visit Frigate Bay:

1. Beaches: Frigate Bay is famous for its beautiful beaches, which have immaculate white sand and crystal-clear turquoise waters. South Frigate Bay Beach, commonly known as "The Strip," is a bustling length of sand that is dotted with beach bars, restaurants, and resorts. North Frigate Bay Beach, also known as Timothy Beach, has a more tranquil and peaceful ambiance that is ideal for sunbathing, swimming, and water sports.

2. Water Sports: Frigate Bay is a water sports enthusiast's paradise. Snorkeling, scuba diving, kayaking, jet skiing, and paddleboarding are among the activities available. The

tranquil waters and abundance of marine life make it an excellent location for exploring the vivid undersea world.

3. Golf: The Royal St. Kitts Golf Club, an 18-hole championship course, is located at Frigate Bay. Golfers may enjoy a round of golf amid lush tropical scenery with spectacular views of the Caribbean Sea and adjacent islands.

4. Frigate Bay comes alive at night with a thriving entertainment scene. The neighborhood is densely packed with beach bars, cafes, and clubs where you can listen to live music, dance to Caribbean rhythms, and savor delectable cocktails. The Strip is well-known for its vibrant nightlife, which features a mix of local and international talent.

5. Restaurants and Dining: Frigate Bay has a diverse range of restaurants and eateries that cater to a wide range of tastes. There are lots of options to tickle your taste buds, ranging from seaside barbecues providing fresh seafood to up market dining venues serving international and local cuisines.

6. Shopping: There are various shopping malls and boutiques in Frigate Bay where you can purchase everything from local handicrafts and souvenirs to designer clothing and jewelry. Take a stroll through the retail sections and peruse the offerings, which include distinctive Caribbean-inspired clothes and artwork.

7. Relaxation and Wellness: Frigate Bay also provides opportunities for renewal and relaxation. Pamper yourself with a spa treatment, take a yoga session on the beach, or simply relax and enjoy the quiet atmosphere of the area.

Frigate Bay holds a number of events and festivals throughout the year, including beach parties, music festivals, and cultural celebrations. Check the local calendar to see if any intriguing activities are scheduled during your visit.

Frigate Bay is a busy and energetic St. Kitts location that offers the ideal combination of sun, sand, water sports, nightlife, and leisure. Frigate Bay provides something for everyone, whether you're looking for adventure, cultural activities, or simply a spot to relax and enjoy the beauty of the Caribbean.

Beaches and Water Sports

St. Kitts and Nevis have beautiful beaches and a variety of water activities for guests to enjoy. Here are some of the best beaches and water activities in St. Kitts and Nevis, whether you're looking for relaxation on the smooth sand or adventure in the turquoise waters:

1. South Frigate Bay Beach (The Strip): South Frigate Bay Beach is a busy and popular location on St. Kitts' southeastern shore. Beach bars, restaurants, and resorts border the beach, creating a lively environment. Relax on the sandy sand, cool off in the warm Caribbean Sea, or try water activities like jet skiing, paddleboarding, and snorkeling.

2. North Frigate Bay Beach (Timothy Beach): A short walk from South Frigate Bay Beach, North Frigate Bay Beach offers a more calm and relaxed atmosphere. The calm waves of this gorgeous beach make it excellent for swimming and sunbathing. Take a stroll along the beach or relax in the shade of the palm trees.

3. Pinney's Beach: Pinney's Beach is a beautiful expanse of golden sand that stretches for miles on the island of Nevis. The beach has a serene and uncrowded ambience that is ideal for lengthy walks or sunbathing. Along the beach, you can also locate beach bars and restaurants where you may try local food and sip refreshing drinks.

4. Cockleshell Bay: Located on St. Kitts' southern edge, Cockleshell Bay is a lovely beach with a laid-back feel. The beach has beautiful views of Nevis and pristine waves with nice sand. Water sports such as snorkeling, paddle boarding,

and kayaking are popular here. You can also take a short boat journey to Shitten Bay, which has colorful coral reefs.

5. Oualie Beach: Located on the island of Nevis, Oualie Beach is a picturesque and secluded area with a peaceful environment. The beach is recognized for its calm waves, which make swimming and snorkeling excellent. It's also a popular launching location for boat cruises, fishing excursions, and sailing excursions.

6. Water Sports: For those looking for excitement, St. Kitts & Nevis has a plethora of water sports activities. Explore the vivid underwater environment brimming with colorful coral reefs and marine life by snorkeling or scuba diving. For those looking for an adrenaline rush on the water, jet skiing, kayaking, paddleboarding, and kiteboarding are all popular options.

7. Tours by Catamaran and Boat: Take a catamaran or boat tour around the islands to explore the beaches, visit isolated coves, and snorkel in clear waters. These cruises frequently include stops at lovely beaches, swimming and sunbathing opportunities, and even sightings of dolphins and sea turtles.

8. Deep-Sea Fishing: If you enjoy fishing, St. Kitts and Nevis has some of the best deep-sea fishing in the world. Charter a

fishing boat and set out to sea in quest of marlin, tuna, mahi-mahi, and other game species.

Whether you're seeking for relaxation, water sports, or underwater experiences, St. Kitts and Nevis' beaches and water activities offer countless possibilities to enjoy the Caribbean's spectacular natural beauty and warm waters.

Beach in South Frigate Bay

South Frigate Bay Beach, popularly known as "The Strip," is a popular and bustling beach on St. Kitts' southeast coast. It has a bustling ambiance with lovely sandy shoreline, crystal-clear waters, and a variety of services. Here's what to expect if you go to South Frigate Bay Beach:

1. Immaculate Beach: South Frigate Bay's beach is noted for its immaculate beauty. The fine golden sand is ideal for relaxing, sunning, and constructing sandcastles. The lovely blue waters beckon you to swim or simply wade in the calm waves.

2. South Frigate Bay Beach is dotted with beach bars, restaurants, and resorts that provide a busy and exciting ambiance. Delicious Caribbean cuisine, tropical beverages, and local delicacies are available. Many restaurants and bars

provide beachside seating, allowing you to enjoy your meal or drink while overlooking the water.

3. South Frigate Bay Beach has a variety of water sports activities for those looking for adventure. Rent a jet ski and race across the waves, try paddleboarding to explore the shoreline, or go snorkeling to see the underwater world, which is filled with colorful fish and coral reefs. Kiteboarding is also popular on the beach, which has great wind conditions for this thrilling water sport.

4. Beach Volleyball: South Frigate Bay Beach is a popular destination for beach volleyball players. On the sand, you can frequently find friendly matches or organized tournaments. Join in or simply watch the exciting games if you're looking for some energetic fun.

5. Beachfront Lounging: Many resorts and beach restaurants along South Frigate Bay Beach serve their visitors with beach loungers and umbrellas. These amenities can be rented so that you can rest in comfort while soaking up the sun and admiring the beautiful beach surroundings.

6. South Frigate Bay Beach is well-known for its raucous beach parties and activities. The beach comes alive with music, dancing, and festivities during peak seasons and

special occasions. It's a terrific way to meet locals and other travelers while taking in the bright Caribbean vibe.

7. Sunset Views: South Frigate Bay Beach has spectacular sunset views. As the day comes to an end, the sky becomes a canvas of vibrant colors, providing a beautiful and picturesque environment. Find a vantage point on the beach or at a beachside bar to watch the sunset and take unforgettable shots.

South Frigate Bay Beach in St. Kitts is a lively and active area where you can enjoy the best of sun, sand, water sports, and beachside eating. This beach has something for everyone, whether you're looking for relaxation, adventure, or mingling.

Cockleshell Cove

Cockleshell Bay is a gorgeous and calm beach on St. Kitts' southern tip. It is well-known for its natural beauty, tranquil waters, and breathtaking views of Nevis Island. Cockleshell Bay is the ideal beach spot for anyone seeking a tranquil and serene beach experience. Here's what to expect if you go to Cockleshell Bay:

1. Cockleshell Bay is surrounded by amazing natural beauty. The beach is bordered by lush flora and swaying palm palms and is embellished with lovely white sand. The Caribbean Sea's blue waves contrast beautifully with the sandy shoreline, creating a picture-perfect environment.

2. Cockleshell Bay offers a more quiet and peaceful setting than some of the busier beaches on the island. Because the beach is less busy, you may enjoy a more tranquil and relaxed beach experience. It's a perfect location for individuals looking for peace and quiet.

3. Crystal Clear Waters: Cockleshell Bay's waters are quiet and clear, making it ideal for swimming and snorkeling. Take a refreshing dip in the warm Caribbean Sea or rent snorkeling equipment to explore the vivid underwater environment. You'll see a variety of brightly colored fish, coral reefs, and other aquatic life.

4. Water Sports: While Cockleshell Bay is famed for its peace and quiet, it also provides chances for water sports lovers. Rent kayaks or paddleboards and glide around the tranquil waters while taking in the scenery. Because of the ideal wind conditions, the bay is also a popular site for kiteboarding.

5. Sunbathing and relaxation: Cockleshell Bay is a wonderful beach for sunbathing and relaxing. Find a nice location on

the soft sand, spread out your beach towel or rent a beach chair, and relax in the warm Caribbean sun. You can genuinely rejuvenate and take in the peacefulness with the serene ambiance and gorgeous natural surrounds.

6. Beachfront Dining: Cockleshell Bay has various beachfront restaurants and bars where you can enjoy delectable Caribbean food while taking in panoramic views of the bay. Enjoy fresh seafood, tropical beverages, and other regional favorites while relaxing on the beach.

7. The breathtaking view of Nevis Island across the ocean is one of the highlights of Cockleshell Bay. While relaxing on the beach or dining at one of the beachside restaurants, you may take in the lush green mountains and stunning coastline of Nevis. The vista is especially beautiful during daybreak and sunset.

8. Boat Excursions: Cockleshell Bay serves as a jumping off place for a variety of boat excursions and cruises. You may take a lovely boat ride around the coast, visit adjacent islands, or even go on a catamaran tour to explore the nearby waterways. These boat excursions frequently include snorkeling, swimming, and wildlife observations.

In St. Kitts, Cockleshell Bay provides a tranquil and lovely beach experience. It's the ideal spot for leisure, aquatic activities, and interacting with nature, thanks to its pure beauty, calm ambience, and breathtaking vistas.

Beach in North Frigate Bay

North Frigate Bay Beach, also known as Timothy Beach, is a lovely and peaceful beach on St. Kitts' southeastern shore. It has a more relaxed ambience than its noisier neighbor, South Frigate Bay Beach. Here's what to expect if you go to North Frigate Bay Beach:

1. North Frigate Bay Beach is recognized for its serene and tranquil atmosphere. The beach is less crowded, making for a more peaceful and relaxing atmosphere. It's ideal for anyone looking for a more personal beach experience and a calm refuge away from the masses.

2. North Frigate Bay's beach is characterized by silky, golden sand that runs for a great distance. It's excellent for long walks, creating sandcastles, or simply relaxing in the shade of a palm tree. You can relax on the sand while listening to the calm murmur of the waves.

3. North Frigate Bay's waters are tranquil and welcoming, making it ideal for swimming and wading. Because of the

lack of strong currents and waves, it is a safe and entertaining beach for families and people of all swimming levels. Swim leisurely in the warm Caribbean Sea or float on the soothing waves.

4. Snorkeling: While North Frigate Bay lacks the large coral reefs found in other snorkeling destinations, there are still chances for underwater exploration. Snorkeling near the beach's rocky portions can show colorful fish, sea turtles, and other marine life. It's an excellent choice for individuals who want to explore the underwater environment without going too far from shore.

5. Beachfront Dining: There are a number of beachfront restaurants and cafes along the beach that give wonderful views of the sea. Enjoy wonderful Caribbean cuisine, fresh seafood, and tropical beverages while relaxing on the beach. It's the ideal place to unwind, dine, and take in the scenery.

6. North Frigate Bay Beach has a variety of waterfront activities for guests to enjoy. You may explore the shoreline at your own speed by renting kayaks or paddleboards. Furthermore, some local operators may provide boat tours or fishing expeditions departing from the shore, allowing for additional exploration and excitement.

7. Romantic Sunsets: The beach in North Frigate Bay is an excellent vantage point for viewing spectacular sunsets. The sky becomes a canvas of bright colors as the sun sets below the horizon, creating a beautiful and mystical mood. It's a fantastic time to take a walk along the beach or sit on the sand and enjoy nature's amazing display.

North Frigate Bay Beach on the island of St. Kitts provides a serene and tranquil beach experience. It's the ideal spot to unwind, connect with nature, and enjoy the serenity of the Caribbean, with its soft sand, calm waves, and laid-back environment.

The Turtle Beach

Turtle Beach, located on St. Kitts' southern coast, is a picturesque and unspoiled beach recognized for its natural beauty and as a nesting site for endangered sea turtles. Here's what to expect if you go to Turtle Beach:

1. Turtle Beach is a remote and pristine length of shoreline that offers a serene and unspoiled ambience. The beach provides a wonderful setting for relaxation and exploration, surrounded by thick vegetation and bordered by the pure blue waters of the Caribbean Sea.

2. Turtle Beach is a key nesting area for sea turtles, especially the endangered leatherback turtles, as the name suggests. During nesting season, which usually lasts from March to November, you may be able to witness the extraordinary sight of sea turtles coming ashore to lay their eggs. Witnessing the nesting process or watching baby turtles hatch and make their way to sea is an unforgettable experience.

3. Soft Sand and Calm Waters: The beach has soft, golden sand that is ideal for sunbathing, sandcastle building, or simply wandering along the shoreline. The waters are tranquil and welcoming, making swimming both safe and fun. You can swim in the crystal-clear seas or simply rest on the beach while listening to the relaxing murmur of the waves.

4. Snorkeling and Diving: Turtle Beach has excellent snorkeling and diving. The seas around the beach are home to colorful coral reefs that are filled with marine life. Take your snorkeling or scuba gear and explore the underwater world, where you'll see colorful fish, sea turtles, and other intriguing species.

5. Natural Beauty & Wildlife: Turtle Beach is surrounded by natural beauty and different ecosystems beyond the beach.

Take a stroll down the beach and look at the coastal flora and fauna. Coastal birds, hermit crabs, and other small critters may be encountered. Keep a look out for iguanas, which have been spotted in the neighborhood.

6. Turtle Beach provides a tranquil and serene ambiance away from people and commercial development. It's great for people looking for a peaceful and isolated beach experience. Turtle Beach is the ideal location for relaxing under a palm tree, taking a leisurely stroll down the sand, or simply enjoying the serenity.

7. Turtle Beach contributes to ongoing conservation efforts to safeguard sea turtles and their nesting sites. Local organizations monitor and protect nesting turtles in order to ensure their survival for future generations. Visiting Turtle Beach makes you realize how important it is to protect these magnificent creatures and their habitat.

Because nesting turtles are so sensitive, it is critical to respect their territory and follow any standards or regulations in place to protect them. When seeing sea turtles, always visit with a reputable tour operator or follow the advice of local conservation organizations.

In St. Kitts, Turtle Beach provides a one-of-a-kind and environmentally significant experience. It's a beach location that blends relaxation with a deeper respect for marine conservation, thanks to its natural beauty, nesting sea turtles, and quiet ambiance.

Friars Bay, South

South Friars Bay, on St. Kitts' western coast, is a gorgeous beach recognized for its natural beauty, tranquil waves, and relaxed environment. Here's what to expect when you visit South Friars Bay:

1. South Friars Bay is surrounded by amazing natural beauty. The beach is set amid beautiful green hills and provides breathtaking views of the Caribbean Sea. The silky white sand and turquoise waves offer a gorgeous scene ideal for relaxation and enjoyment.

2. South Friars Bay has a more tranquil and relaxed vibe when compared to other of the busier beaches on the island. It is less busy, making it a perfect location for individuals seeking peace & quiet. South Friars Bay is a tranquil retreat where you may relax, read a book, or simply soak up the sun.

3. Swimming and Snorkeling: South Friars Bay's waters are quiet and inviting, making it a safe and pleasurable

swimming beach. The gradual slope of the seabed keeps the water shallow for a long distance, making it appropriate for even new swimmers. Snorkeling is especially popular here because the pristine waters provide for close-up views of colorful fish and coral reefs.

4. Beachside Dining and Bars: There are various beachside restaurants and bars in South Friars Bay where you may enjoy great Caribbean cuisine and cool drinks. Many restaurants provide oceanfront seating, allowing you to dine while overlooking the water. While enjoying the pleasant coastal wind, you can experience local delicacies, fresh seafood, and tropical beverages.

5. Water Sports and Activities: For those looking for excitement, South Friars Bay provides a range of water sports and activities. You may explore the coastline by renting kayaks or paddleboards, or you can try your hand at windsurfing. The bay is also a famous site for jet skiing, parasailing, and boat cruises, offering spectacular aquatic adventures.

6. Hammocks and Beach Loungers: There are spots along the beach with hammocks and beach loungers where you may relax and unwind. Relax, feel the gentle sway of the hammock, and take in the tranquility of your surroundings.

You can rent beach chairs and umbrellas for a more comfortable day at the beach.

7. Sunset Views: South Friars Bay provides beautiful views of the Caribbean Sea at sunset. The sky changes into a stunning rainbow of hues as the sun sets, creating a magical and romantic environment. Watching the sunset from the beach is a must-do activity that will provide you with an unforgettable moment throughout your visit.

South Friars Bay is a St. Kitts hidden gem that offers a calm and gorgeous beach experience. Whether you're looking for leisure, water sports, or simply admiring nature's beauty, this beach provides the ideal environment for a great day by the sea.

Pump Bay on Saint Kitts

Pump Bay is a small black sand beach in Sandy Point Town on St. Kitts' west coast. The bay is popular for snorkeling and diving since it is home to a variety of coral reefs and species. Swimming and sunbathing are additional popular activities on the beach.

Pump Bay is roughly 5 kilometers from Basseterre's capital city. The beach has no public transit, thus the best way to reach there is by car or cab. The beach has a modest parking lot, but it can fill up quickly on busy days.

There is no admission cost to the beach, which is open to the public. There are a few food and drink vendors on the beach, but if you plan on spending the day there, bring your own snacks and drinks.

Pump Bay is a lovely and secluded beach ideal for a relaxing day in the sun. Pump Bay is an excellent choice for a more private beach experience.

Wildlife and Nature

St. Kitts and Nevis are endowed with immense natural beauty and diverse animals, making them a perfect destination for nature lovers and wildlife aficionados. Here are some examples of nature and wildlife experiences available in St. Kitts and Nevis:

1. Exploration in the Rainforest: The islands are home to rich rainforests that provide wonderful chances for exploration. Take a guided trek through the rainforest paths to see the flora and fauna, which includes towering trees, vivid tropical flowers, and unique bird species.

2. Mount Liamuiga Volcano: Mount Liamuiga is a dormant volcano in the Caribbean island of St. Kitts. Take a strenuous but rewarding walk to the peak, where you'll be rewarded with panoramic views of the surrounding islands and crater lake. Along the walk, you may discover rare plant species as well as monkeys and other wildlife.

3. Brimstone Hill Fortress National Park: Brimstone Hill Fortress is a UNESCO World Heritage Site with both historical and environmental value. The park is situated on a hilltop and offers stunning views of the coastline and the beautiful green surroundings. The location is ideal for birding, as it is home to a variety of bird species.

4. St. Kitts and Nevis are key nesting places for endangered sea turtles such as the leatherback, hawksbill, and green turtles. During nesting season, guided excursions are available to watch the nesting process or the hatching of baby turtles. Local organizations seek to safeguard these priceless creatures and provide conservation education.

5. Botanical Gardens: St. Kitts has lovely botanical gardens that display the island's diverse plant life. Discover a vast range of tropical plants, including exotic flowers, towering palm trees, and medicinal herbs, in the well-kept gardens. The gardens also serve as a haven for native bird species.

6. Marine Life and Snorkeling: The waters of St. Kitts and Nevis are rich with marine life, making it a snorkeling and scuba diving paradise. Explore bright coral reefs, swim with tropical fish, and possibly even sea turtles and rays. To truly appreciate the underwater world, you can join boat cruises or visit designated snorkeling sites.

7. Rainforest Canopy Tours: A rainforest canopy tour is an amazing excursion. Fly through the treetops on ziplines and suspension bridges for an unforgettable view of the rainforest. Keep an eye out for monkeys, birds, and other creatures that inhabit the treetops as you fly through the canopy.

8. Pelican Cove and Narrows: Pelican Cove and Narrows are scenic spots on the southeastern coast of Nevis where you may enjoy calm beach walks, soak up the sun, and observe the natural beauty of the coastline. Keep a look out for the area's resident pelicans and other shorebirds.

These are just a few of the environment and wildlife adventures on offer in St. Kitts and Nevis. Whether you prefer hiking through rainforests, discovering marine habitats, or simply admiring the beauty of the islands' surroundings, there will be plenty of opportunity to connect with nature and see unique species throughout your visit.

Liamuiga Mountain

Mount Liamuiga, commonly known as Mount Misery, is St. Kitts and Nevis' highest point, rising 3,792 feet (1,156 meters) above sea level. It is a dormant volcano that provides adventurers and nature lovers with a fascinating and gratifying hiking experience. Here's what to expect if you hike Mount Liamuiga:

1. Hiking Mount Liamuiga is a difficult effort that requires a good level of fitness and stamina. The trek is steep at times and challenging, but the spectacular views and sense of success make it worthwhile. It is recommended that you hire a local guide to accompany you and assure your safety throughout the trip.

2. Scenic Beauty: Ascending Mount Liamuiga will reward you with breathtaking vistas of the surrounding countryside. St. Kitts and Nevis' lush jungle, flowing waterfalls, and panoramic panoramas provide for a gorgeous environment. Take in the grandeur of the mountain's unique flora and fauna, which includes tropical plants, bright flowers, and a diversity of bird species.

3. Crater Lake: At the peak of Mount Liamuiga, you'll find a beautiful crater lake known as the "Liamuiga Crater." This

deep, emerald lake is tucked within the caldera of the extinct volcano and adds an intriguing touch to the trek. It's a one-of-a-kind sight that offers a quiet and peaceful setting for a well-deserved respite.

4. Natural and geological wonders: Hiking Mount Liamuiga allows you to see amazing geological features. You may come across lava formations, volcanic boulders, and other evidence of the volcano's activity along the walk. It's an intriguing approach to learn about the geological history of the island and comprehend the forces that sculpted the scenery.

5. Flora and Fauna: A wide variety of plant and animal species can be found on Mount Liamuiga. As you walk the trail, you may come across ferns, orchids, and bromeliads, among other tropical plants. Several bird species, including hummingbirds, bananaquits, and thrushes, live in the dense rainforest. Keep a watch out for monkeys, particularly the vervet monkey, which is prevalent in the area.

6. Guided Tours: When hiking Mount Liamuiga, it is highly advised that you take a guided tour. Local guides are well-versed in the trail, safety procedures, and natural beauties to be found along the way. They can also provide valuable

insights on the mountain's history, geology, and ecology, enriching your overall experience.

7. Weather Considerations: When planning your hike, it's critical to keep the weather in mind. The peak is frequently blanketed in clouds, and rain falls frequently in the rainforest. It is best to check the weather forecast and dress appropriately, including rain gear and strong hiking shoes.

Hiking Mount Liamuiga is an exciting excursion that allows you to immerse yourself in St. Kitts and Nevis' natural beauty and geological mysteries. It provides an opportunity to physically test oneself while being rewarded with beautiful views and a greater respect for the island's natural heritage.

Black Stones

Black Rocks is a natural feature on St. Kitts' northeastern shore, near the settlement of Saddlers. It is a beautiful geological feature composed of big volcanic boulders and black volcanic rock cliffs. Here's what to expect if you go to Black Rocks:

1. Black Rocks is a geological wonder formed by volcanic action millions of years ago. Basalt, a dark-colored volcanic

rock that gives the area its distinct appearance, is used to make the rocks and cliffs. The contrast between the black cliffs and the pounding waves and azure waters is stunning.

2. Vistas of the Atlantic Ocean: The craggy coastline of Black Rocks provides breathtaking vistas of the Atlantic Ocean. The combination of rushing waves, steep cliffs, and black boulders creates a magnificent image. It's an excellent location for photographing nature's raw splendor.

3. Historical Importance: Black Rocks is historically significant to the island of St. Kitts. This spot is thought to have been utilized as a meeting place and a site for spiritual ceremonies by enslaved Africans transported to the island during the colonial era. The site commemorates the island's history and cultural heritage.

5. Peaceful and Tranquil Environment: Because Black Rocks is not as well-known as some of the island's other tourist attractions, it is a peaceful and tranquil area to visit. The lack of visitors offers for a more tranquil experience, where you can take in the beauty of nature and listen to the roaring waves.

6. Coastal Walks and Exploration: There are coastal walks and exploration options at Black Rocks. You can walk down the rocky shoreline, carefully navigating the boulders, and

enjoy the scenery. Keep an eye out for slippery areas, especially if the rocks are damp.

Black Rocks is well-known for its spectacular sunsets. The sky lights up in vivid shades of orange, pink, and purple as the sun sets beyond the horizon, producing a magnificent glow over the black rocks and the water. It's a wonderful location to unwind and take in the beauty of nature as the day draws to a close.

When visiting Black Rocks, it is critical to take caution and be aware of the strong ocean currents. Swimming is not encouraged in this location due to the powerful waves. However, the natural beauty and distinctive geological features of Black Rocks make it a great stop for those looking for a more calm and off-the-beaten-path experience on St. Kitts.

Wingfield Manor

Wingfield Estate is a historic estate in St. Kitts that provides insight into the island's colonial history. It is an important cultural and historical landmark that allows visitors to learn about the island's sugar industry, slavery, and the lifestyles of plantation owners and workers. Here's what to expect when you visit Wingfield Estate:

1. Wingfield Estate was one of St. Kitts' oldest and largest sugar estates, dating back to the 18th century. It dates back to the 17th century, during the height of sugar production. The estate was an important part of the island's economy and a center of agricultural activities. Exploring the property allows you to learn about the rich history of the sugar industry and its impact on the development of the island.

2. Plantation Great House: The Plantation Great House is the estate's focal point. This magnificent structure housed the plantation owner and functioned as the estate's administrative hub. With its architecture, furnishings, and artifacts, it has been restored to its former splendour and provides a look into colonial life today.

3. Rum Distillery: Wingfield Estate is home to the Caribbean's oldest functioning rum distillery. The distillery uses traditional ways to make high-quality rum. Visitors can join guided tours to learn about the rum-making process, from sugarcane harvesting through distillation and aging. Of course, you'll be able to sample some of the exquisite rums produced on-site.

4. Wingfield Estate has magnificently planted botanical gardens that showcase the island's tropical vegetation. You'll see a variety of plant types as you walk through the gardens, including brilliant flowers, exotic trees, and aromatic herbs. It's a beautiful and tranquil area, ideal for a leisurely stroll or a moment of rest.

5. Interpretive Center and Museum: The estate has an interpretive center and museum that provide information about the plantation's history as well as the lives of those who lived and worked there. Exhibits, displays, and interactive presentations provide a thorough overview of the plantation's history, including the experiences of the estate's enslaved Africans.

6. Wingfield Estate offers guided tours that provide guests with in-depth information about the plantation's history and significance. Experienced guides will lead you through the estate's numerous regions, providing stories, anecdotes, and historical context. Their knowledge and experience augment the tour by adding depth and context.

7. Picnic sites and Scenic Views: Wingfield Estate has picnic sites where you can have a leisurely lunch surrounded by beautiful scenery. There are additional vantage places that

offer picturesque views of the rolling hills, the Caribbean Sea, and the lush greenery, making for wonderful photographs.

Wingfield Estate offers an enthralling excursion into St. Kitts' colonial past, combining history, culture, and natural beauty. It's a site where you may explore the relics of the sugar business, learn about the lives of individuals who worked on the plantation, and enjoy the beautiful sceneries of the island. Wingfield Estate is a one-of-a-kind and instructive experience that you should not miss while in St. Kitts.

Nevis Botanical Gardens

The Botanical Gardens of Nevis, also known as the Nevis Botanical Gardens and Montpelier Gardens, are a spectacular natural beauty oasis located on the Caribbean island of Nevis. These beautiful gardens provide a tranquil and enchanting experience, allowing visitors to immerse themselves in the bright vegetation and quiet environs of the island. Here's what to expect when visiting the Nevis Botanical Gardens:

1. Diverse Plant Life: The Botanical Gardens of Nevis showcase the island's rich botanical heritage with a diverse

array of tropical plants and flowers. You'll see a wide range of palm trees, orchids, hibiscus, heliconias, and other exotic plants. The grounds have been meticulously planted, resulting in a vibrant and appealing environment.

2. The gardens are set on the grounds of the historic Montpelier Estate, a former sugar plantation. The estate was built in the 18th century and has kept its colonial beauty. Exploring the gardens allows you to travel back in time and understand the site's historical significance.

3. Japanese Gardens: The magnificent Japanese Gardens are one of the Botanical Gardens' features. Traditional Japanese themes such as peaceful ponds, beautiful bridges, and meticulously kept bonsai trees may be seen in these meticulously created gardens. The serene setting and Zen-like atmosphere make it an ideal location for rest and contemplation.

4. Tropical Rainforest Walk: The Botanical Gardens of Nevis have a nature route that leads you through a miniature tropical rainforest. You'll be surrounded by towering trees, thick vegetation, and the pleasant sounds of birds chirping as you meander along the trail. It's an opportunity to reconnect with nature and enjoy the island's natural beauty.

5. Herb and Medicinal Garden: There is also a herb and medicinal garden in the gardens where you may learn about the traditional usage of various plants for health and wellness. Learn about the medicinal characteristics of native plants and their importance in traditional Caribbean medicine.

6. Views: From the gardens, visitors may take in stunning views of the Nevis countryside, the adjacent Nevis Peak, and the glittering Caribbean Sea. Take a moment to appreciate the beauty of your surroundings and take memorable photos.

7. Dining and refreshments are available in the Botanical Gardens of Nevis, which has a delightful open-air restaurant serving delectable Caribbean food. While enjoying the serene environment of the gardens, indulge in local foods and cool beverages.

Before you depart, stop by the gift shop, where you'll find a variety of locally manufactured crafts, artwork, and botanical products. Take a bit of Nevis home as a souvenir of your visit.

The Botanical Gardens of Nevis offer a peaceful respite from the stresses of everyday life. These gardens are a delight to visit whether you are a nature lover, a horticulture aficionado, or simply looking for a calm refuge. (((Indulge yourself in the magnificence of the))) island's flora, relax in the peaceful settings, and admire Nevis' rich botanical heritage.

Mount Nevis

Nevis Peak is the beautiful centerpiece of the Caribbean island of Nevis. It is an iconic landmark with stunning vistas and exhilarating hiking opportunities, rising to a height of approximately 3,232 feet (985 meters). Here's what to expect when visiting Nevis Peak:

1. Nevis Peak is bordered by lush rainforests and beautiful meadows, giving a scenic environment. Ascending the peak provides panoramic views of the island, the Caribbean Sea, and nearby islands. The area's natural splendor is just breathtaking, making it a haven for nature enthusiasts and photographers.

2. Hiking journey: Climbing Mount Nevis is an exciting and hard journey that draws hikers from all over the world. The hike usually lasts several hours and needs moderate to high fitness. The trail can be steep, difficult, and slippery at times. Hiring a local guide who is familiar with the terrain and can ensure your safety is suggested.

3. Nevis Peak is home to a wide variety of plant and animal species. The lush rainforest on the mountain is filled with tropical flora, including ferns, orchids, bromeliads, and towering trees. Various bird species, including hummingbirds, banana quits, and warblers, benefit from the profusion of greenery. Other species to look out for includes monkeys, lizards, and colorful butterflies.

4. Unique Geological Formation: Nevis Peak is a dormant volcano, and trekking to its summit allows you to see the region's fascinating geological features. Volcanic rocks, lava deposits, and relics of prior eruptions characterize the mountain. It's an enthralling opportunity to learn about the volcanic history of the island and appreciate the forces that sculpted its environment.

5. Weather Considerations: When planning your trek to Nevis Peak, take the weather into account. The mountain is frequently shrouded in clouds, and rain is prevalent in the jungle. Check the weather forecast, dress correctly in lightweight, moisture-wicking clothing, and carry along necessary supplies such as sunscreen, bug repellant, and plenty of water.

6. Reaching the summit of Nevis Peak is a satisfying experience that provides a sense of success as well as a

profound connection with nature. Standing on top of the mountain, with the island stretching out below you, you'll receive a fresh perspective and appreciation for the Caribbean's majesty and grandeur.

7. Local Culture and History: For the inhabitants of Nevis, Nevis Peak is culturally and historically significant. The mountain is revered by the island's indigenous and Afro-Caribbean people, and its genesis is the subject of numerous tales and stories. Exploring Nevis Peak allows you to learn about the island's cultural past and spiritual ties to the natural surroundings.

Hiking Nevis Peak is an unforgettable trip that immerses you in the spectacular natural sceneries of Nevis. It provides a unique opportunity to connect with nature, experience the island's biodiversity, and enjoy the geological wonders of the region, with tough paths and spectacular viewpoints.

The Narrows

The Narrows is a short waterway in the Caribbean that separates the islands of St. Kitts and Nevis. It is a mesmerizing natural wonder that provides tourists with a one-of-a-kind experience. Here's what to expect when visiting The Narrows:

1. The Narrows' magnificent landscape includes crystal-clear blue waterways and lush green hillsides. You'll be treated to panoramic vistas of both St. Kitts and Nevis as you sail or cruise across this strait, providing a lovely backdrop for your adventure. The Narrows' peaceful and tranquil waters provide a serene ambiance ideal for relaxation and enjoyment.

2. Sailing and boating: The Narrows is a popular destination for sailors and boaters. Whether you charter a private boat, take a guided tour, or board a catamaran, sailing The Narrows provides a unique perspective of the islands. You can enjoy the cool sea wind, the warm Caribbean sun, and the natural beauty of the surroundings.

3. Snorkeling and Diving: The Narrows' beautiful waters make it an ideal place for snorkeling and diving. Discover vivid coral reefs, tropical fish, and other aquatic life as you explore the undersea world. Snorkeling or diving in The Narrows allows you to see the Caribbean's vibrant and rich marine ecology.

4. Tranquility and relaxation: The Narrows' tranquil ambiance gives a getaway from the hurry and bustle of daily

life. The tranquil surroundings and quiet seas make for a great backdrop for relaxation. You can unwind and bask in the natural beauty of the area by finding a quiet spot on a beach or onboard a boat.

5. Beaches and Picnic Areas: On both the St. Kitts and Nevis sides of the Narrows, there are several magnificent beaches. These natural beaches are ideal for picnics, sunbathing, and admiring the coastal beauty. Pack a beach towel, some snacks, and a nice book for a relaxing day by the ocean.

6. Species Spotting: The Narrows is home to a diverse range of species. Keep an eye out for seabirds soaring above the lake, such as pelicans and frigate birds. If you're lucky, you might see sea turtles, dolphins, and even whales. The Narrows offers a once-in-a-lifetime opportunity to observe these amazing creatures' native habitats and activities.

7. Sunsets: The Narrows is well-known for its spectacular sunsets. As the day comes to an end, the sky begins to glow with brilliant hues of orange, pink, and purple. Witnessing a sunset in The Narrows is a wonderful experience that should not be missed, whether you're on a boat or enjoying the view from a beach.

Exploring The Narrows provides an enthralling combination of natural beauty, tranquility, and adventure. This strait between St. Kitts and Nevis gives an amazing experience that shows the bucolic charm of the Caribbean, whether you're sailing, snorkeling, or simply enjoying the picturesque surroundings.

Andrea Townson

CHAPTER FOUR

Exploring Nevis

Nevis, one of the two smaller islands that comprise the republic of Nevis and St. Kitts, is a Caribbean hidden gem. Nevis, known for its unspoilt natural beauty, rich history, and kind friendliness, provides guests with a one-of-a-kind and captivating experience. Here are some points to keep in mind when visiting Nevis:

1. Charlestown: Charlestown, the picturesque capital of Nevis, is a delightful town with a laid-back vibe and well-preserved colonial architecture. Take a walk down the cobblestone streets, visit the local market, and explore the old buildings to learn about the island's culture and history.

2. Plantation Houses on Nevis: Nevis is home to several stately plantation houses that offer a look into the island's colonial past. The most notable of these is the Alexander Hamilton House, where the United States' founding father was born. Visit these wonderfully restored houses to learn about its historical significance and to take in the breathtaking scenery.

3. Nevis Peak: Set out on an excursion to the peak of Nevis Peak, a dormant volcano and the island's highest point.

Hiking to the peak provides amazing views of the surrounding landscapes as well as the opportunity to explore the thick rainforest of the island. While the hike can be difficult, the breathtaking panoramic views make it well worth the effort.

4. Nevis Botanical Gardens: Visit the Nevis Botanical Gardens to learn about the island's colorful flora. Explore the meticulously maintained gardens, which feature a diverse range of tropical plants, flowers, and trees. Don't miss the Japanese Garden and the herb and medicinal garden, where you may learn about the traditional usage of plants for healing on the island.

5. Beaches on Nevis: Nevis has natural, uncrowded beaches that are ideal for relaxation and aquatic activities. Pinney's Beach, with its long stretch of silky white sand and crystal-clear seas, is the most popular. Other lovely beaches in the area are Lover's Beach, Oualie Beach, and Nisbet Beach. Spend your days sunbathing, swimming, snorkeling, or simply relaxing on these lovely beaches.

6. Nevis Peak Rum Distillery: A visit to the Nevis Peak Rum Distillery is a must for rum fans. Learn about the rum-making process, from fermentation to aging, on a tour of the

distillery. Try different types of rum and buy a bottle or two as a tasty souvenir of your Nevis vacation.

7. The Historical and Conservation Society of Nevis: Visit the Historical and Conservation Society of Nevis to learn about the island's history and conservation activities. The museum and historical sites on the island are managed by the society, which includes the Institute of Nevis Heritage, the Horatio Nelson Museum, and the Spring House and Bath Hotel. Explore these sites to learn about the history of Nevis and its dedication to protecting its natural and cultural assets.

8. Cultural Events in Nevis: Nevis is well-known for its vibrant cultural events and festivals. Immerse yourself in the colorful music, dance, and local cuisine for an amazing experience if you happen to be on the island during one of these events, such as Culturama or the Nevis Mango & Food Festival.

Discovering Nevis is a journey of discovery, relaxation, and immersion in the rich history and natural beauty of the island. Nevis offers a quiet and authentic Caribbean experience that will leave you with cherished memories, from its beautiful capital to its stunning beaches and lush surroundings.

The Historic Capital of Charlestown

Charlestown, Nevis' ancient capital, is a picturesque town that elegantly displays the island's rich history and colonial past. Charlestown, with its well-preserved architecture, cobblestone streets, and welcoming environment, offers a glimpse into the past while still providing modern-day conveniences and attractions. Here are some of the highlights of this charming town:

1. Georgian Architecture: Take a stroll around Charlestown's streets and marvel at the town's distinctive Georgian-style architecture. Many of the structures are from the 18th and 19th centuries, and they have colorful facades, wooden shutters, and attractive verandas. The town's beautiful architecture lends a touch of elegance and creates a distinct ambiance.

2. The Institute of Nevis Heritage: The Institute of Nevis Heritage is housed in a classic Georgian edifice. takes visitors on a fascinating trip through the island's history. Explore the exhibitions that highlight Nevis' history and culture, such as the island's indigenous past, the colonial era, and its most famous son, Alexander Hamilton. Learn about Nevis' role in the sugar business, the slave trade, and the emancipation struggle.

3. The Alexander Hamilton House: Tour the birthplace of Alexander Hamilton, a founding father of America and the first Secretary of the Treasury. The restored Georgian-style mansion depicts Hamilton's early years and houses antiques and displays connected to his life and accomplishments. It is a must-see for history lovers and Hamilton aficionados.

4. Charlestown Market: At the Charlestown Market, you may immerse yourself in the vibrant local culture. A lively atmosphere awaits you here, with vendors selling fresh fruits and vegetables, spices, and homemade crafts. Immerse yourself in the Caribbean's colors, scents, and flavors by interacting with friendly people and sampling some of the island's bounty.

5. St. Paul's Anglican Church: Take in the magnificent architecture of St. Paul's Anglican Church, one of the Caribbean's oldest churches. This medieval church, built in 1830, has a beautiful white facade and a picturesque cemetery surrounding it. Step inside to enjoy the tranquil environment and the stunning stained glass windows.

6. The Treasury Building: Located in the center of Charlestown, the Treasury Building is an iconic monument that embodies the town's historical significance. This neoclassical-style structure once housed the Nevis Island

Administration and currently houses government offices. It is worth a visit because of its magnificence and historical significance.

7. Galleries and Boutiques: Visit the galleries and boutiques in Charlestown to learn about the local art scene. There is a wide variety of artwork, local crafts, and one-of-a-kind souvenirs that encapsulate the soul of Nevis. Support local craftsmen and bring a bit of Nevis' creativity and craftsmanship home with you.

8. Local Cuisine: Charlestown has a number of restaurants where you may sample real Nevisian cuisine. Try local favorites like goat water, a delicious stew, or freshly caught fish cooked in traditional Caribbean fashions. To round out your dining experience, try a cool rum punch or a local fruit juice.

The historic charm, architectural splendor, and cultural diversity of Charlestown make it a must-see site on the island of Nevis. Charlestown is likely to leave a lasting impression and take you back in time to the island's colonial past, whether you're touring the town's historical monuments, engaging with the friendly residents, or simply soaking up the laid-back environment.

The Museum of Alexander Hamilton

The Alexander Hamilton Museum in Charlestown, Nevis, is an enthralling site that honors the life and legacy of Alexander Hamilton, one of America's founding fathers. The museum, which is housed in the historic building where Hamilton was born in 1755, provides an intriguing view into his early years and the impact he had on forming the United States. Here's what to expect when you go to the Alexander Hamilton Museum:

1. Alexander Hamilton's Birthplace: Step into history as you enter the birthplace of Alexander Hamilton. The museum displays the two-room wooden house where Hamilton spent his boyhood. Immerse yourself in the authentic setting and imagine this influential figure's early years.

2. Exhibits & Artifacts: Take a look at the museum's exhibits, which include a wide range of artifacts, papers, and displays linked to Alexander Hamilton's life. The exhibitions, which include personal belongings and authentic letters as well as copies of historical documents, provide unique insights into Hamilton's journey from Nevis to becoming a key role in American history.

3. Hamilton's Early Life and Education: Learn more about Hamilton's upbringing and education on Nevis. Learn about his mixed-race ancestry, his orphanage, and the influential persons who impacted his childhood. Discover how these formative experiences shaped his later accomplishments.

4. The museum not only analyzes Hamilton's life, but it also shows the historical, cultural, and economic background of Nevis and the Caribbean at the time. Learn about the sugar industry, slavery, and the social dynamics of the region, which will give you a better picture of the world in which Hamilton grew up.

5. Immerse yourself in interactive displays that bring Hamilton's narrative to life. Multimedia presentations, audio recordings, and visual exhibits enhance the tourist experience and make the museum visit instructive and entertaining for visitors of all ages.

6. Take advantage of guided tours led by knowledgeable staff who provide authoritative commentary on Hamilton's life and the relevance of the museum's exhibits. The crew is enthusiastic about presenting Alexander Hamilton's history and legacy and is accessible to answer any questions you may have.

7. Gift store: Browse the museum's gift store for one-of-a-kind Hamilton-related souvenirs and collectibles. You can take home a remembrance of your visit, from books and postcards to Hamilton-themed products, and continue your research of Hamilton's legacy.

The Alexander Hamilton Museum provides an exceptional opportunity to learn about the early life and achievements of one of America's most prominent figures. By visiting Hamilton's birthplace and viewing the exhibits, you'll obtain a better understanding of his legacy and the historical setting in which he lived. Whether you're a history buff or just interested about Alexander Hamilton's life, this museum is a must-see on the island of Nevis.

The Nevis Heritage and Preservation Society

The NHCS (Nevis Historical and Conservation Society is an organization dedicated to conserving and promoting the island of Nevis's unique history, cultural heritage, and natural environment. The NHCS provides visitors with a unique opportunity to explore and appreciate the island's heritage as well as its commitment to sustainability through its different sites, museums, and conservation activities.

Here are some of the highlights of a visit to the Nevis Historical and Conservation Society:

1. The Museum of Nevis History, located in Charlestown, presents a thorough account of Nevis' history. Visitors can learn about the island's indigenous past, the introduction of Europeans, the sugar plantation era, and the struggle for independence through exhibits, antiques, and interactive displays. The museum provides insightful information about the various cultural influences that have shaped Nevis throughout its history.

2. The Horatio Nelson Museum, housed in Captain Horatio Nelson's former townhouse, provides an intriguing peek into the life of the legendary British naval hero. Explore the displays that highlight Nelson's naval career, his ties to Nevis, and his influence on the Caribbean throughout the colonial era. The museum offers a unique look at the island's marine history.

3. Visit the Bath Hotel and Spring House, a well-preserved 18th-century edifice that originally operated as a magnificent retreat for wealthy tourists seeking the medicinal effects of the local hot springs. Take a guided tour of the site to learn about its history and to explore the natural springs that still flow today.

4. Botanical Gardens of Nevis: The NHCS is in charge of the Botanical Gardens of Nevis, a lush and peaceful oasis near Charlestown. Explore the gardens, which are beautifully designed and feature a broad range of tropical plants, flowers, and trees. Take a stroll down the twisting walks, visit the Japanese Garden, and explore the herb and medicinal garden. The gardens provide a tranquil haven where you may take in the natural beauty of the island.

5. Conservation Work: The Nevis Historical and Conservation Society work hard to preserve and safeguard the island's natural environment. The NHCS seeks to ensure the sustainability of Nevis' ecosystems and increase awareness about the need of conservation through activities such as coral reef restoration, turtle conservation, and environmental education programs.

6. Cultural Events and seminars: Throughout the year, the NHCS organizes a variety of cultural events, seminars, and educational activities. These activities promote a greater understanding of Nevisian culture and traditions, ranging from traditional music and dance performances to craft demonstrations and historical reenactments. During your visit, check the NHCS calendar for planned activities.

7. Support Local Artists: The NHCS assists local artisans and craftspeople by providing a venue for them to display and sell their work. Visit the gift shops at each of the NHCS locations to find one-of-a-kind handmade products, artworks, and souvenirs that reflect Nevisian culture and benefit the local community.

You can learn more about the history, culture, and natural beauty of Nevis by visiting the Nevis Historical and Conservation Society locations and participating in their events. The NHCS provides a delightful experience that displays the finest of Nevis' past and present, whether you're touring the island's museums, relaxing in the botanical gardens, or learning about conservation activities.

Spring House and Bath Hotel

The Bath Hotel and Spring House is a historic site on the island of Nevis, located in the hamlet of Bath. This magnificent facility, built in the late 18th century, operated as a beautiful hotel and spa, attracting wealthy visitors from all over the world seeking the curative benefits of the adjacent hot springs. The Bath Hotel and Spring House is now a fascinating site that offers a view into the island's colonial past as well as the era of spa tourism. Here are some of the highlights of a visit to Spring House and the Bath Hotel:

1. The Spring House and the Bath Hotel features exquisite Georgian architecture that embodies the elegance and majesty of the time. The structure has a symmetrical form, huge verandas, and lovely masonry. Its well-preserved exterior provides evidence of prior architectural excellence.

2. Explore the rich history of the Bath Hotel and Spring House, which were important players in the island's social and cultural scene during the 18th and 19th centuries. Learn about the hotel's status as a leading wellness destination and its connections to historical people.

3. The natural hot springs lying nearby are the main attraction of the Bath Hotel and Spring House. The mineral-rich waters' medicinal benefits have been recognized for years, and the hotel capitalized on their restorative reputation. Explore the beautifully landscaped gardens and discover the many hot spring pools that are still active today.

4. Guided Tours: The property provides guided tours given by knowledgeable staff who share information about the history, architecture, and significance of the Bath Hotel and Spring House. They will lead you through the many portions

of the building, offering stories and experiences from the past.

5. Exhibits and informative Displays: Exhibits and informative displays inside the Bath Hotel and Spring House provide a fuller knowledge of the site's history and its significance in the development of Nevis as a tourist destination. These exhibits feature antiques, images, and historical information, allowing you to dig into the world of Caribbean spa tourism.

6. Natural Surroundings: The Bath Hotel and Spring House is surrounded by lush grounds and breathtaking views of the island's coastline. Take a time to savor the peaceful mood and take in the beauty of your surroundings.

While the Bath Hotel is no longer in operation, guests can still benefit from the soothing effects of the hot springs. Many people believe that soaking in the mineral-rich waters can be beneficial to both the body and the psyche. Don't pass up the chance to cool off and relax in this one-of-a-kind natural setting.

The Bath Hotel and Spring House provides a unique view into Nevis' colonial heritage as well as the allure of Caribbean spa tourism. A visit to the Bath Hotel and Spring House is guaranteed to create an impact, whether you're interested in history, architecture, or simply seeking a calm and soothing experience. Immerse yourself in a bygone era's elegance and enjoy the natural beauty that has drawn visitors to this wonderful spot for ages.

Nevis History Museum

The Museum of Nevis History is an enthralling site in Charlestown, the island's ancient capital. The museum, housed in a magnificently restored Georgian-style structure, takes visitors on a fascinating trip through the island's history, cultural heritage, and key events. Here's what to expect when you go to the Museum of Nevis History:

1. Exhibits & relics: Upon entering the museum, you will be greeted by a wide variety of exhibits and relics that depict the narrative of Nevis. The exhibitions cover the whole history of the island, from indigenous artifacts and archaeological finds to colonial-era relics and historical records. Discover the island's indigenous origins, European settlement, the era of sugar plantations, and the emancipation movement.

2. One of the Museum of Nevis History's attractions is its dedication to Alexander Hamilton, one of America's founding fathers who was born in Nevis. Explore exhibits

about Hamilton's life, including his childhood on the island, rise to popularity, and contributions to shaping the United States. Discover his incredible journey from a poor origin in Nevis to becoming a pivotal role in American history.

3. Interpretive Exhibits: The museum's interpretive exhibits provide unique insights into the social, economic, and cultural aspects of Nevisian society at various times. Learn more about the island's own character, traditions, and the numerous influences that have impacted its culture throughout the years.

4. Historical Timeline: A chronological timeline at the Museum of Nevis History walks visitors through the island's key historical events. Follow the timeline to get a clear picture of the island's history, including its colonial origins, the impact of slavery, the struggle for freedom, and the island's journey to independence.

5. Audiovisual Presentations: Immerse yourself in Nevis' history with captivating audiovisual presentations. These multimedia displays bring the island's history to life, providing visitors of all ages with a vibrant and participatory experience. Listen to narrations, watch historical footage, and interact with interactive components to learn more about Nevis' history.

6. Before you depart, stop by the museum's gift store, where you may discover a variety of souvenirs, books, and locally made crafts. Take something from Nevis with you to remember your stay and continue your exploration of the island's history and culture.

7. Knowledgeable Staff: The museum's employees are enthusiastic about Nevis' history and legacy. They are on hand to provide more information, answer questions, and provide insights into the exhibitions, expanding your museum experience.

The Museum of Nevis History is a must-see for history buffs and anybody interested in learning about Nevis' rich cultural heritage. The museum brings the island's history to life via fascinating exhibits, relics, and informative displays, creating a deeper appreciation for its significance and contributions to the larger Caribbean region. At the Museum of Nevis History, you may travel back in time and immerse yourself in the captivating narrative of Nevis.

The Cottle Church

Cottle Church is a historic and culturally significant landmark on the Caribbean island of Nevis. This remarkable church, located in the village of Cottle's Church, has considerable historical value and provides tourists with a look into the island's past. What you need to know about Cottle Church is as follows:

1. Cottle Church, also known as St. Thomas' Anglican Church, has a fascinating history dating back to the early nineteenth century. John Cottle, a former slave who achieved his freedom and became a major landowner on Nevis, constructed it in 1824. The church was built using native volcanic stone, and its architectural design blends both African and European traditions.

2. Cottle Church is culturally significant because it shows the resilience, persistence, and spiritual commitment of the island's once enslaved inhabitants. It represents the struggle for freedom and the tenacity of the Nevisian people.

3. Cottle Church's architectural blend of African and European influences is one of its most outstanding features. The building techniques and design aspects represent Afro-Caribbean traditions brought by enslaved Africans, as well as the influence of the European colonial era. The church's

sturdy stone walls and peculiar shape distinguish it as a landmark on the island.

4. Cottle Church has undergone restoration attempts throughout the years to preserve its historical integrity and assure its continued significance. The Nevis Historical and Conservation Society (NHCS) has been actively involved in the site's preservation and upkeep, allowing tourists to see the church as it once was.

5. Spiritual and Cultural Events: Cottle Church is more than simply a historical landmark; it is also a place of worship and a venue for a variety of spiritual and cultural events. Attend a church service or special event to see a dynamic local community come together to honor their heritage and show their faith.

6. Cottle Church offers a quiet and serene ambiance because it is nestled among the lush foliage of Nevis. The surrounds of the church are tranquil, allowing visitors to reflect and contemplate. Take a minute to enjoy the natural beauty of the place and to absorb the sense of history that pervades the location.

7. Guided Tours: Consider attending a guided tour offered by qualified local guides or members of the NHCS when visiting Cottle Church. They can offer vital insights about the

church's history, architecture, and cultural significance, boosting your understanding and enjoyment of this unique site.

Cottle Church displays Nevis's resiliency and cultural heritage. Its historical significance, unique architecture, and peaceful environs make it an enticing location for people interested in learning about the island's history and connecting with its lively present. Visit Cottle Church to immerse yourself in Nevis' rich historical and cultural tapestry.

Nevis' Fort Charles

Fort Charles is a ruined 17th-century British fort on Nevis's southern edge. It was previously one of the most important forts in the Caribbean, intended to safeguard the island from marine invasion.

The fort was constructed in 1665 and was enlarged and strengthened multiple times throughout the following decades. For the most of its history, it was garrisoned by British forces and was involved in multiple conflicts during the Anglo-French wars of the 17th and 18th centuries.

The fort deteriorated in the nineteenth century and was abandoned in the early twentieth century. It is now a famous tourist site with beautiful views of the surrounding area.

The fort is comprised of several interconnecting structures, including a barracks, a powder storage, and a cistern. The fort's walls are still standing, but they are in poor condition. The fort is also densely forested, which contributes to the atmosphere.

Fort Charles is a must-see on any trip to Nevis if you are interested in history or military architecture. It's an intriguing spot to learn about the island's history and to see the ruins of a once-important fort.

Nevis Beaches and Water Sports

Here are some of Nevis's top beaches and water sports:

1. Pinney's Beach is a long, white-sand beach on Nevis's northwest coast. It is one of the island's most popular beaches, recognized for its tranquil, clear seas and gorgeous surroundings. Pinney's Beach is ideal for swimming, sunbathing, and participating in water sports such as snorkeling and windsurfing.

2. Lovers' Beach is a small, quiet beach on Nevis' northeast coast. It can only be reached by boat or a short hike and is famed for its picturesque location and quiet seas. Popular activities include swimming, sunbathing, and snorkeling at Lovers' Beach.

3. Cockleshell Beach is a long, white-sand beach on Nevis's southwest coast. It is well-known for its quiet, protected waters and scenic beauty. Swimming, sunbathing, and water activities like kayaking and paddleboarding are all popular at Cockleshell Beach.

4. The dormant volcano Nevis Peak reaches 3,232 feet (985 meters) above sea level. The views from the peak are stunning, and on a clear day, you can see all the way to St. Kitts. There are various hiking trails that lead to the top of Nevis Peak, and the hike is a terrific way to appreciate the natural beauty of the island.

Here are some Water Activities Available in Nevis:

1. Because of the clean seas and abundance of marine life, snorkeling and diving are popular sports on Nevis. There are various dive spots on the island, such as Pinney's Beach Reef, Lovers' Beach Wall, and the Nevis Wall.

2. Another prominent water recreation on Nevis is sailing. Day sails, sunset sails, and overnight cruises are all available from various sailing charter businesses.

3. Windsurfing is an excellent way to experience the wind and waves on Nevis. On the island, there are various windsurfing schools and rental shops where you may learn to windsurf or rent equipment.

4. Exploring the waters around Nevis by jet ski is a wonderful experience. On the island, there are various jet ski rental firms that can give you with a jet ski and a helmet.

5. Parasailing is an excellent way to see Nevis from above. You'll be towed behind a boat while tethered to a parachute, and you'll get a bird's-eye view of the island.

Gardens and Plantations

St. Kitts and Nevis have various plantations and gardens that showcase the islands' history, horticulture, and natural beauty. Visitors can explore lush landscapes, learn about the islands' agricultural legacy, and admire the rich flora and wildlife at these destinations. Here are some notable plantations and gardens in St. Kitts & Nevis to visit:

Andrea Townson

1. Romney Manor and Gardens: Romney Manor is a historic plantation estate in St. Kitts with exquisite botanical gardens. The estate's main attraction is the legendary Saman Tree, often known as the "Mother Tree," which is thought to be over 400 years old. The gardens are expertly kept and feature a wide range of tropical flora, such as bright flowers, exotic trees, and medicinal herbs.

2. Wingfield Estate: Wingfield Estate is a former sugar plantation in St. Kitts that has been restored into a heritage site. It is located near Basseterre. Learn about the island's sugar producing history by exploring the remnants of the historic estate structures, including the distillery and sugar mill. A magnificent garden with fruit trees, spices, and medicinal plants is also part of the estate.

3. Botanical Gardens of Nevis: The Botanical Gardens, located on Montpelier Estate on the island of Nevis, provide a quiet and captivating experience. This 7-acre tropical oasis is home to orchids, palms, and bromeliads, among other plants and flowers. The gardens also include an Asian water garden collection, a rainforest conservatory, and a medicinal herb garden.

4. The Hermitage Plantation Inn: Located in the mountains of Nevis, The Hermitage is a lovely 17th-century plantation

inn. The home is surrounded by lovely grounds and provides visitors with a calm escape. Discover a wide range of tropical flora in the gardens, including fruit trees, palms, and flowering shrubs. The inn also acts as a platform for local artists and artisans.

5. Montpelier Plantation and Beach: Montpelier Plantation, another old plantation on Nevis, is now an attractive boutique hotel located among beautifully planted gardens. Take a stroll through the grounds, which are filled with brilliant flowers and beautiful trees. In addition, the plantation provides beautiful views of Nevis Peak and the surrounding landscape.

6. Caribelle Batik: Caribelle Batik in St. Kitts is worth a visit for its unique combination of art and nature. This attraction, located in Romney Manor, features a working batik workshop where you can experience the traditional practice of cloth dyeing. The adjacent gardens provide a tranquil setting while showcasing the island's unique vegetation.

Visiting these plantations and gardens gives a rich and immersive experience that allows you to connect with the history, culture, and natural beauty of the islands. These destinations offer a pleasant study of St. Kitts and Nevis' plantation legacy and botanical wonders, whether you're interested in horticulture, history, or simply appreciate being surrounded by beautiful landscapes.

CHAPTER FIVE

Adventures and Activities

For travelers looking for excitement and remarkable experiences, St. Kitts & Nevis has a wealth of activities and adventures to offer. These islands have something for everyone, from exploring lush rainforests to indulging on adventurous outdoor excursions. Here are some of the best things to do and see in St. Kitts and Nevis:

1. Hike Mount Liamuiga: Mount Liamuiga is St. Kitts' highest peak and provides beautiful trekking options. Explore the lush rainforest on a guided hike, marvel at the various flora and wildlife, and be rewarded with breathtaking panoramic views from the summit.

2. Zipline through the Rainforest: Soaring through the treetops on a zipline excursion provides an adrenaline boost. Several tour providers offer zipline courses that allow you to glide through the rainforest canopy while seeing the island's natural beauty from above.

3. ATV or Jeep Safari: Take an ATV or Jeep safari across the mountainous terrains of St. Kitts and Nevis. Follow skilled guides along off-road trails that highlight the islands' stunning vistas, hidden gems, and historical places.

4. Horseback Riding: Take a guided trail ride to discover the beauty of the islands on horseback. Ride along sandy beaches, through lush forests, and across rolling hills, taking in the scenery and connecting with nature.

5. Paddleboarding and kayaking: Rent a kayak or paddleboard and enjoy the gorgeous seas surrounding the islands. Glide down the coast, explore hidden coves, and uncover isolated beaches while taking in the beauty of the Caribbean Sea.

6. Catamaran Cruises: Sail along the coasts of St. Kitts and Nevis on a catamaran cruise. Enjoy the warm Caribbean breeze, relax on the deck, and take in the breathtaking views. Snorkeling stops, beach visits, and delectable onboard meals are all included on some trips.

7. Golfing: Golfers can enjoy a round of golf on St. Kitts and Nevis' world-class golf courses. Tee off against the backdrop of beautiful ocean views and lush surroundings, and put your talents to the test on these picturesque and well-kept courses.

8. Rainforest Tours: Join a rainforest tour to immerse yourself in the natural splendor of the islands. Experienced guides will lead you through impenetrable forests, pointing

out rare plant and animal species and offering information about the ecology and history of the islands.

9. Beautiful Railway trip: Take a beautiful railway trip in St. Kitts, a one-of-a-kind experience that takes you around the island's coastline. On this lovely railway excursion, you may enjoy panoramic vistas, learn about the island's history and culture, and listen to lively Caribbean music.

10. Sunset Cruises: Relax at the end of the day in paradise with a sunset sail. Sail down the coast as the sun begins to set below the horizon, casting a warm glow on the ocean. While enjoying refreshing cocktails and delectable Caribbean cuisine, toast to the beauty of the islands.

These activities and adventures provide exhilarating and unique experiences, allowing you to immerse yourself in St. Kitts and Nevis' natural marvels and rich culture. These islands are sure to give an amazing holiday, whether you're looking for adrenaline-pumping activities or peaceful excursions.

Nature and Hiking Trails

St. Kitts and Nevis are a hiker's paradise, with numerous hiking and nature routes showcasing the islands' natural beauty and magnificent vistas. There are trails for hikers of all skill levels, from lush jungles to high summits. Lace up your hiking boots and prepare to explore the hiking and wildlife routes listed below:

1. Mount Liamuiga: As St. Kitts' highest peak, ascending Mount Liamuiga is a necessity for adventurers. The trail winds through dense rainforest, across rocky terrain, and ultimately to the peak, where you may enjoy panoramic views of the surrounding islands and the Caribbean Sea.

2. Middle Island walk: On Nevis, this picturesque walk provides insight into the island's history and natural treasures. You'll see relics of old sugar plantations, rich foliage, and panoramic views of the coastline as you hike.

3. Monkey Hill Nature walk: Located in Basseterre, this walk offers a mild hike through the jungle, allowing you to see native flora and fauna, including the trail's namesake, Green Vervet monkeys. The walk is well-marked and offers a tranquil retreat into nature.

4. The Booby Hill Trail, located on the southern edge of Saba Rock, Nevis, takes you through the mountainous terrain of the island and gives spectacular views of the coastline. Keep a look out for the Red-footed Booby, which inspired the trail's name.

5. Bloody Point walk: On Nevis, this historical walk takes you through the location where Carib Indians fought European settlers. It's a moderate-level walk that provides historical insights as well as stunning views of the shoreline.

6. The Black Rocks Trail, located on St. Kitts' northeastern shore, leads to an extraordinary creation of volcanic rocks formed by millennia of volcanic activity. It's a short but wonderful journey that allows you to observe nature's raw strength.

7. The Cross Isles Pathway: The Cross Isles Pathway in St. Kitts is a tough and rewarding excursion for more experienced hikers. This track runs the length of the island, from the Atlantic to the Caribbean coasts, and provides breathtaking views, rich flora and wildlife, and a genuine sense of accomplishment.

8. Rainforest Eco-Tours: Take a guided rainforest eco-tour to discover St. Kitts and Nevis' natural marvels. Guides will walk you through lush forests, pointing out unusual plant species, medicinal herbs, and providing insights into the ecology of the islands.

Wear appropriate hiking shoes, pack lots of water, and be prepared for various terrain conditions. Hiking in a group or with a guide is also recommended for safety and to avoid missing out on any hidden jewels along the way. Enjoy the peace and tranquility of the islands' natural sceneries and immerse yourself in the rich biodiversity of St. Kitts and Nevis.

Festivals and Culture in the Community

St. Kitts and Nevis are well-known not only for their beautiful natural scenery, but also for their vibrant local culture and exciting festivities. Immerse yourself in the rich traditions of the region and enjoy the warm welcome of the locals. Here are some highlights of St. Kitts and Nevis's native culture and festivals:

1. Kittitian culture is a synthesis of African, British, and Caribbean elements. Kittitians, the inhabitants, are noted for their friendliness and hospitality. Engage with the people, learn about their traditions, and enjoy the relaxed island lifestyle.

2. Nevisian Culture: The island of Nevis has a distinct cultural legacy. The Nevisians are proud of their history and customs, which are influenced by both African and British cultures. Take the time to visit the island and mingle with the inhabitants to learn about their culture.

3. Music and Dance: Music and dance are important parts of St. Kitts and Nevis culture. The islands have a diverse musical tradition that includes calypso, reggae, soca, and steel pan. During festivals and festivities, you'll typically hear loud music playing in the streets and locals displaying their dance moves.

4. Carnival: One of the most anticipated festivals in St. Kitts and Nevis is Carnival. It is usually held in December and January, and it includes bright parades, vibrant costumes, exciting music, and vigorous dancing. Participate in the festivities, immerse yourself in the bright ambiance, and feel the infectious Carnival spirit.

5. Culturama: Culturama is a festival held in Nevis to commemorate the island's distinct culture and traditions. This week-long celebration takes place in late July and includes parades, pageants, food stalls, traditional dances, and musical performances. It's a fantastic opportunity to see the Nevisian community's diversity and talent.

6. Fisherman's Day is an annual festival conducted in St. Kitts and Nevis to recognize the local fishing community and its economic contribution to the islands. Boat races, fish frying competitions, and displays of traditional fishing skills are all part of the festival. It's an excellent opportunity to

sample fresh seafood and learn about the island's close relationship with the water.

7. Emancipation Day is a significant celebration in St. Kitts and Nevis that commemorates the abolition of slavery. Cultural performances, drumming, singing, storytelling, and reenactments commemorate the challenges and accomplishments of the island's forefathers.

8. Native Cuisine: Try the native cuisine to experience the flavors of St. Kitts and Nevis. Try saltfish and johnny cake, goat water stew, conch fritters, and fresh seafood. Visit local restaurants and food vendors to taste the distinct flavors and spices that distinguish Caribbean cuisine.

St. Kitts and Nevis is home to numerous excellent artists and craftspeople. Discover magnificent paintings, sculptures, pottery, and handmade crafts at local art galleries and craft markets. Take home a one-of-a-kind piece of artwork as a souvenir of your visit.

By immersing yourself in local culture and attending festivals and events, you'll obtain a better knowledge of the vibrant legacy and customs that make St. Kitts and Nevis such a unique destination. Absorb yourself in the local lifestyle, engage with the welcoming inhabitants, and make memories that last a lifetime.

CHAPTER SIX

Entertainment and Dining

St. Kitts and Nevis has a delectable food scene as well as a plethora of entertainment alternatives that will satisfy your taste buds and keep you delighted during your stay. These islands have something for everyone, whether you want to indulge in indigenous delicacies, savor international cuisine, or experience the active nightlife. Here are some highlights of St. Kitts & Nevis' dining and entertainment:

1. Local food: St. Kitts and Nevis' local food will introduce you to the flavors of the Caribbean. Try the grilled lobster, jerk chicken, coconut shrimp, and delectable conch fritters. Traditional foods such as goat water stew, saltfish and johnny cake, and callaloo soup should not be missed. Taste the original flavors and spices of the islands at local eateries, seaside shacks, and restaurants.

2. International Cuisine: St. Kitts and Nevis also has a diverse international eating scene. Cuisines such as Italian, Mediterranean, Asian, and American can be found in everything from fine dining restaurants to casual diners. Many restaurants use fresh, locally obtained ingredients to make tasty dishes that appeal to a wide range of tastes.

2. Beach Bars and Restaurants: The beach bars and restaurants strewn along the coastlines offer a relaxed dining experience. Enjoy delicious seafood while taking in the breathtaking ocean views and the relaxing sound of waves smashing on the shore. Don't forget to sample some cool tropical cocktails or local rum punches.

3. Cultural Shows & Music: Immerse yourself in St. Kitts and Nevis' lively entertainment scene. Attend cultural concerts that feature traditional dances, music, and storytelling. Enjoy the vibrant dance acts that reflect the islands' rich cultural past, as well as the exuberant rhythms of calypso, reggae, and soca music.

4. Nightlife: The nightlife on St. Kitts and Nevis is vibrant, especially in Basseterre and Frigate Bay. Enjoy live music at bars and cafes, dance the night away at clubs, or simply unwind at a seaside venue. To satisfy varied interests, the nightlife offers a blend of Caribbean moods, international sounds, and pleasant atmospheres.

5. Casinos: If you're feeling lucky, visit one of St. Kitts and Nevis' casinos. Play blackjack, poker, roulette, or slot machines. Enjoy the excitement of gaming as well as the colorful environment of the casinos, which frequently feature entertainment performances and live music.

6. Cooking Classes: Participate in cooking classes to learn the secrets of Caribbean food. Join local chefs who will show you how to make traditional meals, tell you about local products, and provide insights into the islands' culinary traditions.

7. Sunset Cruises: Take a sunset cruise to combine meals with spectacular views. Enjoy a romantic dinner on a catamaran or yacht while sailing along the beaches and watching the sunset over the Caribbean Sea. These cruises frequently offer delectable meals, beverages, and live entertainment.

8. Local Festivals and Events: Take advantage of local festivals and events that include food vendors, live music, and cultural performances. Enjoy a range of meals from various vendors, as well as the joyful environment and participation in the celebration of local traditions.

9. Street Food: Check out the local street food scene for excellent nibbles and quick bites. Street food vendors offer a variety of cuisines to delight your taste buds, from savory burgers and grilled meats to tropical fruit smoothies and sweet desserts.

Whether you want a gourmet dining experience, a casual seaside dinner, or an evening of entertainment, St. Kitts and Nevis has a dining and entertainment choice to suit every taste. During your vacation, indulge in the local flavors, explore the exciting nightlife, and create memorable experiences.

Restaurants and Local Cuisine

Some of the local cuisines and restaurants in St. Kitts and Nevis are as follows:

1. St. Kitts and Nevis' national cuisine is saltfish and dumplings. It is cooked using saltfish (dried codfish that has been soaked and rehydrated) and dumplings (flour, water, and salt). Saltfish is usually prepared in a stew with vegetables including onions, tomatoes, and peppers. The dumplings are boiled or steamed before being served with the saltfish stew.

2. Callaloo is a lush green vegetable popular in Caribbean cooking. It's commonly used in soups and stews, but it's also delicious on its own. Callaloo is strong in fiber and a good source of vitamins A and C.

3. Fufu is a dough-like meal made from cassava or plantain. It is often served boiled or steamed with stews or soups. Fufu is a healthy source of carbs and, if cooked with beans or meat, can also be a good source of protein.

4. Jerk chicken: This is a dish of marinated chicken with spices such as allspice, thyme, garlic, and scotch bonnet peppers. The chicken is then grilled or roasted until thoroughly done. Jerk chicken is a popular dish in St. Kitts and Nevis, where it can be found in a variety of restaurants and street food booths.

5. Roti is a type of flatbread made from wheat flour and water. It is usually packed with curried vegetables or meat and folded in half before being grilled on a griddle. Roti is a popular meal in St. Kitts and Nevis, and it can be found in a variety of restaurants and street food booths.

Here are several restaurants in St. Kitts and Nevis that serve native cuisine:

1. Creole Restaurant and Bar: Located in Basseterre, St. Kitts, this restaurant provides classic Caribbean cuisine. Saltfish and dumplings, callaloo, fufu, and jerk chicken are among the items on the menu.

2. Mrs. Moore's Eat to Live Snackette: A popular venue for local cuisine in Basseterre, St. Kitts. The menu includes rotis as well as other Caribbean specialties like curried goat and fried seafood.

3. Weekendz Bar and Grill: Located near Pinney's Beach, Nevis, this restaurant is recognized for its relaxed environment and delicious meals. The menu includes both traditional local cuisine and more international fare such as burgers and pasta dishes.

4. Tiranga Restaurant: Tiranga Restaurant serves Indian food in Charlestown, Nevis. The menu includes tandoori dishes as well as other Indian classics like biryani and naan bread.

5. Sugar Apple Inn: Located in Old Road Town, Nevis, this restaurant serves a range of Caribbean cuisine. Saltfish and dumplings, callaloo, and jerk chicken are among the items on the menu. A popular Sunday brunch buffet is also available at the restaurant.

Cuisine of St. Kitts

Here are some of St. Kitts' most popular dishes:

1. St. Kitts and Nevis' national cuisine is saltfish and dumplings. It is cooked using saltfish (dried codfish that has been soaked and rehydrated) and dumplings (flour, water, and salt). Saltfish is usually prepared in a stew with vegetables including onions, tomatoes, and peppers. The

dumplings are boiled or steamed before being served with the saltfish stew.

2. Callaloo is a lush green vegetable popular in Caribbean cooking. It's commonly used in soups and stews, but it's also delicious on its own. Callaloo is strong in fiber and a good source of vitamins A and C.

3. Fufu is a dough-like meal made from cassava or plantain. It is often served boiled or steamed with stews or soups. Fufu is a healthy source of carbs and, if cooked with beans or meat, can also be a good source of protein.

4. Jerk Chicken: This is a dish of marinated chicken with spices such as allspice, thyme, garlic, and scotch bonnet peppers. The chicken is then grilled or roasted until thoroughly done. Jerk chicken is a popular dish in St. Kitts and Nevis, where it can be found in a variety of restaurants and street food booths.

5. Roti is a type of flatbread made from wheat flour and water. It is usually packed with curried vegetables or meat and folded in half before being grilled on a griddle. Roti is a popular meal in St. Kitts and Nevis, and it can be found in a variety of restaurants and street food booths.

6. Goat Water: A classic soup made with goat meat, vegetables, and spices. It's a filling and savory dish that's usually served with rice or dumplings.

7. Peas and Rice: A basic dish of rice and pigeon peas that is often served with vegetables or meat on the side. It is a satisfying and inexpensive dish popular throughout the Caribbean.

8. Johnnycakes: Johnnycakes are little, flat pastries made from cornmeal and water. Typically, they are cooked in oil and eaten with butter or honey. In St. Kitts and Nevis, Johnnycakes are a popular breakfast item.

9. Sugar Cake: A delicious cake made from molasses, sugar, flour, and spices. It is frequently accompanied by a cup of tea or coffee. In St. Kitts and Nevis, sugar cake is a popular dessert.

These are just a few of the numerous delectable foods available in St. Kitts. Whatever your taste, you will find something to appreciate in our vibrant and eclectic cuisine.

Cuisine from Nevis

The following are some of the most popular foods on Nevis:

1. Goat Water: A classic soup made with goat meat, vegetables, and spices. It's a filling and savory dish that's usually served with rice or dumplings.

2. Roti is a type of flatbread made from wheat flour and water. It is usually packed with curried vegetables or meat and folded in half before being grilled on a griddle. Roti is a popular meal in Nevis, and it can be found in a variety of restaurants and street food carts.

3. Conch Fritters: Conch meat is used to make these little, fried fritters. They're usually accompanied by a dipping sauce, such as ketchup or tartar sauce. In Nevis, conch fritters are a popular appetizer or snack.

4. Sheep Curry: This meal consists of sheep meat cooked in a curry sauce. It's a popular meal on Nevis, usually served with rice or roti.

5. Peas and Rice: A basic dish of rice and pigeon peas that is often served with vegetables or meat on the side. It is a satisfying and inexpensive dish popular throughout the Caribbean.

6. Butter Chicken is a chicken meal that has been marinated in a spice mixture that includes turmeric, ginger, and garlic. Following that, the chicken is cooked in a tomato-based sauce and served with rice or naan bread. In Nevis, butter chicken is a famous meal and is available at a variety of restaurants.

7. Tuna Salad: A basic salad with tuna, mayonnaise, celery, and onions. It is a popular dish in Nevis and is frequently served as a light lunch or dinner.

8. Johnnycakes: Johnnycakes are little, flat pastries made from cornmeal and water. Typically, they are cooked in oil and eaten with butter or honey. Johnnycakes are a popular breakfast item on the islands of Nevis and St. Kitts.

9. Sugar Cake: A delicious cake made from molasses, sugar, flour, and spices. It is frequently accompanied by a cup of tea or coffee. In Nevis and St. Kitts, sugar cake is a favorite dessert.

These are just a few of the numerous delectable foods available in Nevis. Whatever your taste, you will find something to appreciate in our vibrant and eclectic cuisine.

10 Must-Try Local Delights

Here are ten must-try St. Kitts & Nevis delicacies:

1. Saltfish and Dumplings: St. Kitts and Nevis' national cuisine, saltfish and dumplings, is made using dried codfish that has been soaked and rehydrated, as well as dumplings made with flour, water, and salt. Saltfish is usually prepared in a stew with vegetables including onions, tomatoes, and peppers. The dumplings are boiled or steamed before being served with the salt fish stew.

2. A classic soup made with goat meat, veggies, and spices. It's a filling and savory dish that's usually served with rice or dumplings. Slow-cooked goat meat in a broth with vegetables such as carrots, potatoes, and onions. The soup is then seasoned with spices including thyme, allspice, and scotch bonnet peppers.

3. Conch Fritters: Conch meat fritters, small and fried. The Caribbean Sea is home to conch, a species of shellfish. The conch meat is diced and combined with a flour, egg, and spice batter. After that, the batter is fried till golden brown. Conch fritters are usually accompanied by a dipping sauce, such as ketchup or tartar sauce.

4. Roti: A flatbread cooked using wheat flour and water. It is usually packed with curried vegetables or meat and folded in half before being grilled on a griddle. Roti is a popular meal in St. Kitts and Nevis, and it can be found in a variety of restaurants and street food booths.

5. Callaloo is a lush green vegetable popular in Caribbean cooking. It's commonly used in soups and stews, but it's also delicious on its own. Callaloo is strong in fiber and a good source of vitamins A and C.

6. Small patties comprised of mashed fish, veggies, and spices. In St. Kitts and Nevis, fishcakes are a popular snack or appetizer. They're usually deep-fried till golden brown and served with a dipping sauce like ketchup or tartar sauce.

7. Johnnycakes: Johnnycakes are little, flat pastries made from cornmeal and water. Typically, they are cooked in oil and eaten with butter or honey. In St. Kitts and Nevis, Johnnycakes are a popular breakfast item.

8. Molasses, sugar, flour, and spices are used to make a sweet cake known as sugar cake. It is frequently accompanied by a cup of tea or coffee. In St. Kitts and Nevis, sugar cake is a popular dessert.

9. Pepperpot: A traditional meat, pigtails, oxtails, veggies, and spice stew. It's a filling and savory dish that's usually served with rice or dumplings. The stew is slow-cooked for several hours, allowing the flavors to blend.

10. Rum Cake: A luxurious and rich cake made with rum, sugar, flour, and spices. It is frequently accompanied by a scoop of ice cream or a dollop of whipped cream. Rum cake is a famous dish in St. Kitts and Nevis, where it is frequently given as a gift.

11. Sorrel: A typical Caribbean drink made from hibiscus blossoms, sorrel. It's a tangy and refreshing drink that's popular throughout the holidays. Sorrel can be produced with either water, sugar, and spices or rum.

These are just a few of the numerous delectable indigenous foods available in St. Kitts & Nevis. Whatever your taste, you will find something to appreciate in our vibrant and eclectic cuisine.

St. Kitts Must-Try Restaurants

Here are a few must-visit eateries in St. Kitts:

1. Tiranga Restaurant: This Indian cuisine restaurant is popular with both locals and visitors. The menu includes tandoori chicken, butter chicken, and naan bread, among other items.

2. Mrs. Moore's Eat to Live Snackette: This little eatery is well-known for its saltfish and dumplings. The dumplings are freshly made to order, and the saltfish is cooked in a delectable stew.

3. The Boatyard: This beachfront restaurant in Basseterre boasts a great view of the port. The menu includes seafood meals, burgers, and pasta dishes.

4. Sugar Apple Inn: This restaurant provides Caribbean food and is located in Old Road Town on Nevis. The menu includes a range of traditional local foods such as saltfish and dumplings, callaloo, and goat water.

5. Creole Restaurant and Bar: Located in Basseterre, this restaurant provides classic Caribbean cuisine. Roti, conch fritters, and pepperpot are among the foods on the menu.

6. Weekendz Bar and Grill: This casual restaurant is located on Pinney's Beach on Nevis. Burgers, pasta dishes, and shellfish are among the foods on the menu.

7. Sugar Reef Restaurant: Located in Frigate Bay on Nevis, this restaurant provides a great view of the ocean. There are several seafood meals on the menu, as well as steak and chicken dishes.

8. The Old Tavern: This restaurant in Charlestown, Nevis, is popular with both locals and tourists. The menu includes foods such as saltfish and dumplings, goat water, and conch fritters.

These are just a few of the many excellent restaurants to be found in St. Kitts & Nevis. Whatever your taste, you'll find something to enjoy in this bustling and diversified food scene.

Entertainment and Nightlife

Here are some of St. Kitts and Nevis's most popular nightlife and entertainment options:

1. The Strip is a vibrant strip of pubs and clubs in Basseterre, St. Kitts. The Strip is an excellent location for dancing, drinking, and socializing.

2. Mr. X's Shiggidy Shack is a bar and grill in Frigate Bay, Nevis. Mr. X's is well-known for its karaoke and live music nights.

3. Kactus Nightclub is a nightclub in Basseterre, St. Kitts. Cactus is a popular venue for dancing and listening to electronic music.

4. Aqua Lounge & Bar is a bar and lounge in Basseterre, St. Kitts. Aqua Lounge boasts a laid-back environment with wonderful views of the water.

5. Sugar Apple Inn: Located in Old Road Town on Nevis, this restaurant boasts a busy bar scene. Sugar Apple Inn is a favorite hangout for both locals and tourists.

6. The Old Tavern: This restaurant has a small bar area and is located in Charlestown, Nevis. The Old Tavern is a well-known venue for live music and socializing.

These are just a few of the many fantastic nightlife and entertainment options available in St. Kitts and Nevis. Whatever your taste, you will find something to appreciate in this vibrant and diversified atmosphere.

Top Ten Pubs and Nightclubs

The following are the top ten pubs and nightclubs on St. Kitts and Nevis:

1. St. Kitts' Cactus Nightclub: Cactus Nightclub is a famous venue for dancing and listening to electronic music. It may be found in Basseterre, St. Kitts.

2. Basseterre, St. Kitts, The Strip: The Strip is a vibrant strip of pubs and clubs in Basseterre, St. Kitts. It's a fantastic place for dancing, drinking, and mingling.

3. Nevis's Mr. X's Shiggidy Shack: Mr. X's Shiggidy Shack is a restaurant and bar in Frigate Bay, Nevis. It is well-known for its karaoke and live music nights.

4. Nevis Sugar Apple Inn: Sugar Apple Inn is a restaurant with a bustling bar scene in Nevis' Old Road Town. It is a popular destination for both locals and tourists.

5. Nevis's Antique Tavern: The Old Tavern is a restaurant in Charlestown, Nevis, with a small bar area. It is a popular gathering place for live music and socializing.

6. Nevis Reggae Beach Bar & Grill: Reggae Beach Bar & Grill is a beach bar on Nevis's Frigate Bay. It is well-known for its cocktails, food, and live music.

7. Basseterre, St. Kitts, The Boatyard: In St. Kitts, there is a boatyard. The Boatyard is a seaside restaurant in Basseterre, St. Kitts. It has a lovely view of the bay and is a popular seafood restaurant.

8. St. Kitts Ocean Terrace: Ocean Terrace is a seaside pub and restaurant in Basseterre, St. Kitts. It is well-known for its cocktails, food, and live music.

9. St. Kitts and Nevis playground: Playground is a pub and arcade in St. Kitts' Basseterre. It is a popular gathering place for drinks, games, and socializing.

10. The Mongoose Pub is located in St. Kitts. Mongoose bar is a traditional British bar in Basseterre, St. Kitts. It is well-known for its cocktails, food, and live music.

Live Music Venues

The following are some live music venues in St. Kitts and Nevis:

1. The Boatyard in Basseterre, St. Kitts, is a beachfront restaurant with a great view of the harbor. On weekends, they frequently host live music.

2. Ocean Terrace is a waterfront bar and restaurant in Basseterre, St. Kitts, offering a stunning view of the port. On weekends, they frequently host live music.

3. Kactus Nightclub in Basseterre, St. Kitts, is a prominent dance and electronic music venue. On weekends, they frequently host live music.

4. Mr. X's Shiggidy Shack is a pub and grill in Frigate Bay, Nevis, known for its karaoke nights and live music.

5. Sugar Apple Inn is a restaurant with a bustling bar scene in Old Road Town, Nevis. On weekends, they frequently host live music.

6. The Old Tavern is a restaurant with a small bar in Charlestown, Nevis. On weekends, they frequently host live music.

7. Reggae Beach Bar & Grill in Frigate Bay, Nevis, is a busy beach bar. On weekends, they frequently host live music.

8. Playground is a bar and arcade in Basseterre, St. Kitts, providing live music most weekends.

9. Mongoose Pub in Basseterre, St. Kitts, is a British-style pub that features live music on weekends.

These are only a few of St. Kitts and Nevis' many live music venues. Whatever your taste, you will find something to appreciate in this vibrant and diversified atmosphere.

Shopping

Shopping in St. Kitts and Nevis is a unique and diversified experience that allows tourists to bring a bit of the islands' culture and workmanship home with them. Here are some shopping highlights to discover during your vacation, ranging from local crafts and souvenirs to duty-free shopping and premium boutiques:

1. Port Zante: Port Zante, located in Basseterre, is a popular shopping location for both cruise ship passengers and visitors. It has a number of duty-free shops selling luxury things such jewelry, watches, fragrances, and designer clothing. Use the duty-free prices to get excellent bargains on high-end products.

2. The Circus is a lively location in the centre of Basseterre with a roundabout ornamented with Victorian-style clock towers. Local vendors and shops sell handicrafts, artwork, apparel, and souvenirs in this bustling district. Browse the

stalls and shops for one-of-a-kind goods that reflect the local culture and craftsmanship.

3. Pelican Mall: Pelican Mall, located in Basseterre, is a modern shopping complex with a range of stores. Clothing, accessories, gadgets, and local souvenirs are available here. It's a convenient location for shopping for necessities and exploring local offerings.

4. Goods Market: The Crafts Market, located in Port Zante, is a must-see for visitors looking for authentic local goods and souvenirs. Local artisans and vendors sell a variety of handmade things like as ceramics, wood carvings, woven baskets, jewelry, artwork, and batik textiles. Prices are commonly negotiated, so feel free to do so.

5. Charlestown Market: The Charlestown Market in Nevis is a thriving centre for local products and crafts. Explore the stalls and talk to the sellers offering fresh fruits and vegetables, spices, and herbs. Handmade products such as ceramics, baskets, and textiles are also available. The market offers a dynamic setting in which to immerse yourself in local culture.

6. Galleries and Boutiques: There are several art galleries and boutiques on St. Kitts and Nevis that showcase the work of local artists. Visit these galleries to find one-of-a-kind

paintings, sculptures, pottery, and other works of art that reflect the island's beauty and culture. There are also upmarket boutiques selling designer clothing, accessories, and jewelry.

7. Rum Distilleries: St. Kitts and Nevis is well-known for its rum manufacturing, and a visit to a local rum distillery allows you to buy true Caribbean rum. Explore the distilleries, learn about the rum-making process, and peruse the aged rums and flavored variants.

8. Local Food Products: Don't forget to bring home some of St. Kitts & Nevis' delectable delicacies. Look for locally produced food items such as hot sauces, spices, jellies, and tropical fruit preserves. These make excellent gifts or keepsakes, allowing you to taste the flavors of the island long after you return home.

Remember to verify customs restrictions and duty-free allowances before shopping in St. Kitts and Nevis, especially when purchasing luxury items or big quantities of goods. Choose authentic locally manufactured products to support local artisans and businesses. Explore the bustling markets, boutiques, and galleries to locate one-of-a-kind souvenirs that will remind you of your time on these beautiful islands.

Souvenirs and Gifts

Here are some of the top St. Kitts & Nevis souvenirs and presents to buy:

1. Rum: Because St. Kitts and Nevis is famous for its rum, you can't go wrong with purchasing a bottle as a souvenir. Mount Gay, Brinley Gold, and Cockspur are other prominent brands.

2. Handcrafted crafts: St. Kitts and Nevis has many brilliant artisans who create wonderful handcrafted items such as jewelry, pottery, and paintings. These are excellent keepsakes that are not available elsewhere.

3. Local produce: Many tropical fruits and vegetables, such as bananas, mangoes, and pineapples, are grown on St. Kitts and Nevis. Fresh vegetables is available at local markets and roadside kiosks.

4. Coffee and chocolate: St. Kitts and Nevis' coffee and chocolate industries are also growing. Many shops and supermarkets sell locally produced coffee and chocolate.

5. Apparel: Because St. Kitts and Nevis has a relaxed dress code, there is plenty of casual apparel to buy as keepsakes. T-shirts, shorts, and beachwear with the local flag or other Caribbean designs are popular.

6. Souvenir magnets: These are usually popular gifts that come in a variety of shapes and sizes. Magnets with the local flag, landmarks, or other Caribbean motifs are ideal.

8. Keychains: Another popular souvenir item is keychains. Look for keychains featuring the national flag, landmarks, or other Caribbean themes.

These are only a few examples of souvenirs and presents available in St. Kitts & Nevis. Whatever you choose, your friends and family will enjoy a taste of the Caribbean when you return home.

Accessories and Fashion

Sure, outlined are a few of the most well-known. St. Kitts and Nevis clothes and accessories:

1. Rum-inspired apparel: Because St. Kitts and Nevis is famous for its rum, there is no shortage of clothing and accessories with rum-related motifs and designs. T-shirts, hats, backpacks, and other items are included.

2. handcrafted jewelry: St. Kitts and Nevis has many excellent artists that create stunning handcrafted jewelry such as necklaces, bracelets, and earrings. This jewelry is

frequently crafted from materials available locally, such as seashells, coral, and wood.

3. Traditional Caribbean clothes: The traditional dress worn on St. Kitts and Nevis reflects the islands' rich history and culture. This comprises dresses, skirts, and shirts fashioned of vividly colored textiles with traditional patterns.

4. Beachwear is usually popular in St. Kitts and Nevis because it is a tropical location. Swimsuits, cover-ups, and sarongs are all included. Beachwear comes in a variety of forms, sizes, and colors.

5. Souvenir hats: Hats are a popular souvenir item, and they come in a variety of forms and sizes. Look for hats featuring the local flag, monuments, or other Caribbean themes.

6. Keychains: Another popular souvenir item is keychains. Look for keychains featuring the national flag, landmarks, or other Caribbean themes.

These are only a few fashion and accessory options available in St. Kitts and Nevis. Whatever you select, you'll discover something that reflects the island's distinct culture and beauty.

Andrea Townson

CHAPTER SEVEN

Useful Information

It is crucial to have some practical information when visiting St. Kitts and Nevis to guarantee a smooth and pleasurable vacation. Here are some important details to remember:

1. St. Kitts and Nevis follows Atlantic Standard Time (AST), which is four hours behind Greenwich Mean Time (GMT-4). Daylight Saving Time is not observed on the islands.

2. The Eastern Caribbean Currency (XCD) is the national coinage of St. Kitts and Nevis. US currencies, on the other hand, are commonly accepted throughout the islands. ATMs are available in large towns and tourist destinations, and most restaurants take credit cards.

3. Electricity: The standard voltage in St. Kitts and Nevis is 230 volts and the frequency is 60 hertz. The most common plug kinds are Type A and Type B, which are the same as in the United States and Canada. Consider packing a travel adapter if your devices use multiple plug kinds.

4. St. Kitts and Nevis are typically safe places, although precautions should always be taken. Keep an eye on your stuff, especially in crowded places, and avoid wearing expensive jewelry or displaying valuables. It's also a good

idea to use dependable transportation and exercise caution when exploring unknown regions at night.

5. Health and safety: Travel insurance that covers medical expenses is recommended. In St. Kitts and Nevis, tap water is generally safe to drink, however bottled water is easily available if you prefer. Mosquitoes may be prevalent, so apply insect repellent and wear long sleeves and pants, especially around dawn and twilight.

6. Traveling across the islands is relatively simple. Taxis can be found at the airport, hotels, and tourist attractions. Minivans and buses serve as public transportation, providing an inexpensive way to travel between towns and villages. Renting a car is also possible, and driving is done on the left side of the road.

7. Internet and communication: The majority of hotels, restaurants, and cafes provide free Wi-Fi to their guests. Mobile networks cover the islands well, although it's best to check with your service provider about international roaming costs. Purchasing a local SIM card can be a cost-effective choice if you need to make local calls.

8. The climate in St. Kitts and Nevis is tropical, with warm temperatures all year. The wet season lasts from May to November, whereas the dry season lasts from December to

April. To protect oneself from the sun, bring lightweight, breathable clothing, swimsuits, sunscreen, and a hat.

9. Etiquette and customs: It is critical to observe local customs and traditions. Dress modestly and remove your hat when visiting churches or religious locations. It's also nice to greet locals with a warm "Good morning" or "Good afternoon." It's traditional to remove your shoes while entering someone's home.

In an emergency, phone 911 to contact the police, ambulance, or fire services in St. Kitts and Nevis. Keep the contact information for your country's embassy or consulate handy in case you need assistance while traveling.

By remembering these practical elements, you can have a stress-free and delightful time touring the lovely islands of St. Kitts and Nevis.

Accommodation Options

The following are some of the most popular places to stay in St. Kitts and Nevis:

1. The St. Kitts Marriott Resort & Spa is a magnificent resort on the picturesque Grace Bay Beach. It has a spa, various restaurants, and a casino among its features.

2. The Four Seasons Resort Nevis: This premium resort is located on the island of Nevis in a private cove. It provides breathtaking views of the Caribbean Sea as well as a variety of activities such as sailing, snorkeling, and hiking.

3. The Sugar Beach Resort & Spa is located on the island of Nevis, on a white-sand beach. It is recognized for its lavish hotels and a variety of restaurants, pubs, and activities.

4. The Golden Lemon Resort & Spa is situated on a cliff with a view of the Caribbean Sea. It is noted for its breathtaking vistas and calm ambiance, as well as a variety of restaurants, pubs, and activities.

5. The Nisbet Plantation Beach Club is a magnificent beach resort on the island of St. Kitts. It has a wide range of restaurants, pubs, and activities and is recognized for its friendly personnel and laid-back environment.

6. The Kittitian Hill Resort is situated on a hilltop with a view of the Caribbean Sea. It is recognized for its breathtaking vistas and elegant lodgings, as well as a variety of restaurants, pubs, and activities.

7. The Old Manor Hotel is located in the center of Basseterre, St. Kitts. It has a number of restaurants, bars, and stores and is well-known for its pleasant environment and courteous employees.

8. The Plantation Inn is a charming inn in the centre of Charlestown, Nevis. It is noted for its historic charm and courteous employees, as well as a variety of restaurants, pubs, and stores.

These are just a few of the many wonderful locations to reside in St. Kitts & Nevis. Whatever your budget or style, you will find the ideal location to stay on these gorgeous islands.

Hotels and Resorts

Here are a few of the best hotels and resorts in St. Kitts:

1. The St. Kitts Marriott Resort & Spa is located on the picturesque Grace Bay Beach. It has a spa, various restaurants, and a casino among its features.

2. The Royal St. Kitts Hotel & Casino is a five-star resort on Frigate Bay. It provides breathtaking views of the Caribbean

Sea as well as a variety of activities such as golf, tennis, and water sports.

3. The Sugar Beach Resort & Spa is located on the island of Nevis, on a white-sand beach. It is recognized for its lavish hotels and a variety of restaurants, pubs, and activities.

4. The Golden Lemon Resort & Spa is situated on a cliff with a view of the Caribbean Sea. It is noted for its breathtaking vistas and calm ambiance, as well as a variety of restaurants, pubs, and activities.

5. The Nisbet Ranch Surf Club is a magnificent beach hamlet on the barrier reef of St. Kitts. It has a wide range of restaurants, pubs, and activities and is recognized for its friendly personnel and laid-back environment.

6. The Kittitian Hill Resort is situated on a hilltop with a view of the Caribbean Sea. It is recognized for its breathtaking vistas and elegant lodgings, as well as a variety of restaurants, pubs, and activities.

8. The Old Manor Hotel is located in the center of Basseterre, St. Kitts. It has a number of restaurants, bars, and stores and is well-known for its pleasant environment and courteous employees.

The Plantation Inn is a charming inn in the centre of Charlestown, Nevis. It is noted for its historic charm and courteous employees, as well as a variety of restaurants, pubs, and stores.

These are only a few of the many excellent hotels and resorts on St. Kitts. Whatever your budget or style, you will find the ideal location to stay on these gorgeous islands.

Bed and Breakfasts

Here are some highly rated St. Kitts guesthouses and B&Bs:

1. The Inn at Pelican Beach: On the island of St. Kitts, this guesthouse is set on a magnificent beach. It has a pool, a restaurant, and a bar as well as other amenities.

2. The Cliffside Inn is perched on a cliff overlooking the Caribbean Sea. It has beautiful scenery and a range of activities such as hiking, snorkeling, and kayaking.

3. The Old Sugar Mill Inn is a bed and breakfast in the heart of Basseterre, St. Kitts. It has a pleasant environment and numerous amenities, such as a pool, a restaurant, and a bar.

4. The Golden Pineapple Inn is located on the island of St. Kitts in the settlement of Old Road. It provides a tranquil

and relaxing ambiance as well as a variety of amenities such as a pool, a restaurant, and a bar.

5. The Old Manor Inn is located in the center of Charlestown, Nevis. It has a pleasant environment and numerous amenities, such as a pool, a restaurant, and a bar.

6. The Montpelier Inn is situated on a hilltop with a view of the Caribbean Sea. It has beautiful scenery and a range of activities such as hiking, biking, and horseback riding.

7. The Nisbet Plantation Inn is situated on a lovely beach on the island of St. Kitts. It has a pool, a restaurant, and a bar as well as other amenities.

These are just a few of the many wonderful guesthouses and bed and breakfasts on St. Kitts and Nevis. Whatever your budget or style, you will find the ideal location to stay on these gorgeous islands.

Vacation Rentals and Villas

Here are some of the most popular villas and vacation rentals in St. Kitts and Nevis:

1. Belle Mont Farm: On the island of St. Kitts, this villa is located on a functioning farm. It features breathtaking views

of the Caribbean Sea as well as a pool, a hot tub, and a tennis court.

2. Villa Kiani: On the island of Nevis, this villa is perched on a cliff overlooking the Caribbean Sea. It has beautiful views and a range of amenities, such as a pool, a hot tub, and a private beach.

3. Sugar Reef home: On the island of Nevis, this home is positioned on a magnificent beach. It has a pool, a hot tub, and a private chef among its many facilities.

4. Oceanside - 2 Bedroom - Marriott Beach Club: This vacation rental is located on St. Kitts' gorgeous Grace Bay Beach. It features breathtaking views of the Caribbean Sea as well as a pool, a hot tub, and a fitness center.

5. Sealofts On The Beach: This vacation property on the island of Nevis is set on a gorgeous beach. It has several amenities, including a pool, a hot tub, and a private terrace with breathtaking views of the Caribbean Sea.

6. The Montpelier Inn: On the island of Nevis, this inn is perched on a hilltop overlooking the Caribbean Sea. It has beautiful scenery and a range of activities such as hiking, biking, and horseback riding.

7. Nisbet Plantation Beach Club: On the island of St. Kitts, this inn is set on a magnificent beach. It has a pool, a restaurant, and a bar as well as other amenities.

8. The Inn at Pelican Beach: On the island of St. Kitts, this guesthouse is set on a magnificent beach. It has a pool, a restaurant, and a bar as well as other amenities.

These are just a few of the many wonderful villas and vacation rentals available in St. Kitts & Nevis. Whatever your budget or style, you will find the ideal location to stay on these gorgeous islands.

Eco-Lodges and Camping

Some of the top camping and eco-lodges in St. Kitts and Nevis are as follows:

1. Nevis Estate Plantation: On the island of Nevis, this eco-lodge is built on a thriving plantation. It provides incredible views of the Caribbean Sea as well as a variety of activities such as hiking, biking, and horseback riding.

2. The Hermitage is an eco-lodge amid the jungle on the island of Nevis. It offers breathtaking rainforest vistas as well

as a variety of activities such as hiking, birdwatching, and swimming in natural pools.

3. Pirates Bay Campground: On the island of St. Kitts, this campground is set on a magnificent beach. It provides breathtaking views of the Caribbean Sea as well as a variety of activities such as swimming, snorkeling, and sunbathing.

4. Islander's Beach Club: On the island of St. Kitts, this eco-lodge is set on a magnificent beach. It provides breathtaking views of the Caribbean Sea as well as a variety of activities such as swimming, snorkeling, and sunbathing.

5. Conservation and Development Trust: On the island of St. Kitts, this group organizes camping and trekking tours. They have a wide range of paths to select from, ranging from easy to difficult.

6. Nevis Peak Adventure: On the island of Nevis, this company offers camping and trekking adventures. They have a wide range of paths to select from, ranging from easy to difficult.

These are just a few of the fantastic camping and eco-lodges available in St. Kitts & Nevis. Whatever your budget or style, you will find the ideal location to stay on these gorgeous islands.

CHAPTER EIGHT

Tips for Safety and Security

Here are some travel safety and security tips for St. Kitts and Nevis:

1. Keep an eye on your surroundings, especially at night, when crime rates tend to be greater.

2. If you must carry substantial sums of cash or jewels, keep them in a secure location, such as a hotel safe.

3. Don't leave anything unattended, including your luggage, wallets, and phones.

4. Drive with caution: the roads in St. Kitts and Nevis can be small and winding, and the speed limit is frequently disobeyed.

5. Swim in specified places and be aware of the situations prior to joining the water. There are strong currents and rip tides in some areas, so it is vital to swim in designated areas and be aware of the situations prior to joining the water.

6. Drinking too much alcohol might affect your judgment and make you more susceptible to crime.

7. Trust your instincts: If you feel unsafe, don't be afraid to leave.

Here are some more St. Kitts and Nevis-specific recommendations:

1. Be wary of stealing: Petty theft is the most common crime in St. Kitts and Nevis.

2. ATM skimming should be avoided: There have been reports of ATM skimming devices being installed on ATMs in St. Kitts and Nevis.

3. Be wary of the possibility of sexual assault: Sexual assault is a major issue in St. Kitts and Nevis. Please notify the police immediately if you are a victim of sexual assault.

4. Be aware of the risk of human trafficking: Human trafficking is a severe problem in St. Kitts and Nevis. Please notify the police immediately if you feel someone is being trafficked.

It is vital to note that these are only suggestions, and that each scenario is unique. If in doubt, it is usually better to err on the side of caution.

Transportation by Public

Minivans and buses dominate public transit in St. Kitts and Nevis, making it an economical and convenient means to go about the islands. What you should know about public transit is as follows:

1. Minivans: Minivans, also known as "vans" by locals, are the main means of public transportation. They follow predetermined itineraries and can be flagged down along the way. Minivans are identified by a special license plate prefix that indicates they are part of the public transit system. Individuals often own and run these vans on their own.

2. Bus Stops: While minivans can be waved down anywhere along their route, major cities and villages have dedicated bus stops where you can wait for a van. Look for signage indicating the bus stop or ask a local for help. A bus stop is usually identified by a sign or a shelter.

3. Fare Payment: Minivan fares are normally fixed and paid in cash. To pay for your journey, bring small amounts of Eastern Caribbean dollars (XCD). The exact fee may vary based on the distance traveled, although for popular routes, drivers usually have a set charge. Before boarding, it's a good idea to confirm the fare with the driver.

4. Timing: Minivans run on a schedule, however they don't always leave at the same time. They usually wait until the van is full before leaving, so expect a brief wait. Vans can be more numerous at peak hours, particularly in the morning and late afternoon. Outside of these hours, however, the frequency may be lower, so plan appropriately.

5. Minivans typically show their destination on the windshield or side windows. If you have any doubts regarding the route, you can seek confirmation from the driver or other passengers. Locals are usually pleasant and willing to help guests with directions and bus route information.

6. Limited travel in Some locations: While minivans cover most major towns and tourist locations, travel to more distant or less populous areas may be limited. In such instances, alternative mobility choices such as taxis or rented cars should be considered.

7. Bus station: A bus station is located near Independence Square in Basseterre, St. Kitts' capital. This is where you'll find a bigger concentration of minivans and buses departing for various island destinations.

When taking public transit, keep in mind that vehicles might become crowded, particularly during peak hours. Expect a busy and buzzing atmosphere. Also, keep in mind that public transit may have limited evening hours, so plan your trips accordingly.

Using public transportation in St. Kitts and Nevis can be an authentic and cost-effective way to immerse yourself in the local culture and engage with the welcoming islanders. Take advantage of the chance to travel like a local and enjoy the magnificent sights as you visit the islands.

Taxis and Car Rentals are Available

Taxis and vehicle rentals are common modes of transportation in St. Kitts and Nevis, providing passengers with ease and flexibility. What you need to know about taxis and automobile rentals is as follows:

1. Taxis:

Taxis are easily accessible at airports, big hotels, and tourist destinations. Taxis are easily identified by their distinctive license plates, which frequently begin with "TX." Taxis are also available for private hire, allowing you to organize transportation for certain lengths of time or places.

- Charges: Taxi charges in St. Kitts and Nevis are regulated, and popular routes usually have a fixed rate. However, it is best to confirm the fare with the driver before beginning the route. Negotiate the price up front if you need many stops or a prolonged period of time. Tipping is optional but appreciated for excellent service.

- Taxi Associations: There are several taxi associations in St. Kitts and Nevis. Because each association has its own set of rules and prices, fares may differ slightly from one another. To ensure a seamless experience, become acquainted with the taxi association in the region where you will be staying.

2. Rental Cars:

- Rental Car Agencies: Several car rental agencies are available in St. Kitts and Nevis, both at airports and in main towns. It's essential to book ahead of time, especially during high tourist season, to ensure availability and the best pricing. Rental firms provide a variety of car alternatives to meet a variety of demands and budgets.

- Requirements: You must have a valid driver's license from your home country and be at least 25 years old to rent a car. Some agencies will accept drivers as young as 21, but will demand a fee. A valid credit card is required for the rental deposit and insurance purposes.

- Driving: Like the United Kingdom, St. Kitts and Nevis drive on the left side of the road. Take extra precautions and pay attention to road signs and traffic restrictions if you're not used to it. The road infrastructure is generally in good condition, although expect some winding and narrow roads, particularly in more rural areas.

- When renting a car, it is suggested that you have enough auto insurance coverage. Although most rental agencies include basic insurance, you may want to consider obtaining additional coverage for peace of mind. Before signing, go over the rental agreement's terms and conditions as well as the insurance coverage.

- Gas Stations: While gas stations can be found across the islands, it's a good idea to refuel whenever you come across one, especially if you want to travel to more distant locations. Remember that petrol prices may be more than you're used to, so plan accordingly.

Taxis and rented automobiles are both convenient ways to get around St. Kitts and Nevis. When picking between the two options, consider your personal travel demands, budget, and desired amount of independence. Whatever you choose, you'll have the flexibility to explore the islands' stunning landscapes, sights, and local culture at your leisure.

Walking and Cycling

Cycling and walking are both good methods to see St. Kitts and Nevis' gorgeous landscapes and rich culture. What you need to know regarding riding and walking on these islands is as follows:

1. Cycling:

- Bicycle Rentals: Bicycles are available for rent at several rental shops and hotels in St. Kitts and Nevis. This is an excellent alternative for taking your time visiting the islands, taking in the landscape, and immersing yourself in the local culture. Some rental stores may offer guided bike tours or suggest popular routes.

- Road Conditions: Although the road infrastructure in St. Kitts and Nevis is generally well-maintained, it is vital to know that road conditions may vary. While most major roads are in decent condition, some rural areas or less-traveled routes may have uneven surfaces or potholes. Be cautious and mindful of your surroundings.

- Considerations for Safety: When cycling, it is critical to wear a helmet and follow all traffic laws. Be aware of oncoming traffic and keep visible by wearing luminous clothes, especially in low-light settings. Plan your routes ahead of time, taking into account things such as traffic, topography, and fitness level.

- Cycling Routes: St. Kitts and Nevis has a number of scenic routes for bikers. Consider riding along the coast for spectacular ocean vistas, or exploring the interior of the islands for lush foliage and tiny settlements. The Southeast Peninsula in St. Kitts and the Nevis Main Road, which encircle the entire island of Nevis, are two popular routes.

2. Walking:

- Pedestrian-Friendly locations: Many locations in St. Kitts and Nevis, particularly in town centers and tourism destinations, are pedestrian-friendly. On foot, you may explore picturesque streets, browse small stores, and soak up the colorful atmosphere. Walking allows you to take in the views at your own leisure, engage with the locals, and find hidden gems.

- Walking in St. Kitts and Nevis is typically safe, however it is always advisable to use caution. Keep an eye on your surroundings, especially in less busy locations or at night. To reduce the danger of theft or unwelcome attention, stay on well-lit and busy areas and avoid exhibiting costly objects.

- Hiking paths: Both islands provide a range of hiking paths that display the gorgeous scenery and diverse animals for nature enthusiasts and adventure seekers. Popular hiking sites include Mount Liamuiga in St. Kitts and Nevis Peak in Nevis. Hiking with a guide or joining organized hiking trips is recommended to secure your safety and make the most of your experience.

When walking through residential areas or passing through local communities, it is polite to greet the residents with a friendly "Good morning" or "Good afternoon." The locals are known for their warm hospitality, and engaging in a friendly conversation can enhance your cultural experience.

Whether you ride or walk, remember to remain hydrated, wear comfortable shoes, and pack necessary materials such as sunscreen, insect repellant, and a map or navigation system. Always be cautious of wildlife and protected places, and obey any guidelines or restrictions that may be in place.

Exploring St. Kitts and Nevis by foot or bicycle allows you to admire the natural beauty, mingle with the inhabitants, and create lasting memories of your time on these beautiful islands.

Services for Boats and Ferries

Boat and ferry services provide handy transit choices for visiting other Caribbean islands as well as going between St. Kitts and Nevis. What you need to know about boat and ferry services is as follows:

1. Ferries between islands:

- Connection to St. Kitts and Nevis: Regular ferry services connect St. Kitts and Nevis. These ferries run between Basseterre, St. Kitts' capital, and Charlestown, Nevis' capital. The boat voyage takes 45 minutes to an hour, depending on sea conditions and vessel type.

- The Sea Bridge Ferry is the principal ferry operator connecting St. Kitts and Nevis. They provide scheduled services on a regular basis, with many departures throughout the day. It is best to check the ferry schedule ahead of time and arrive at the ferry station early to ensure a seat.

- Ticketing and Fares: Inter-island ferry tickets can be purchased at the ferry port or from approved ticket agents. The costs are reasonable, and it is advised to purchase your tickets in advance, especially during high travel months.

- Island hopping: St. Kitts and Nevis act as gateways to other Caribbean islands. Ferry services to places such as Antigua, St. Maarten, and St. Barth's are available. These services provide options for day trips or longer vacations to discover the region's various beauties.

2. Chartering a Private Boat:

- Private Yachts and Boat Charters: Private boat charters and yacht rentals are available for individuals looking for a more personalized experience. You may personalize your route and explore the islands and surrounding waterways at your leisure with these services. Local tour providers or boat rental firms can help you arrange private charters.

- Island Excursions: Boat trips and excursions on St. Kitts and Nevis are popular pastimes. These tours include snorkeling, diving, fishing, and exploring isolated coves and beaches. Many tour providers offer half-day or full-day outings, with group tours or private charters available.

- Considerations for Safety: When embarking on boat cruises or excursions, it is critical to emphasize safety. Check that the boat or charter firm has all of the required licenses and certifications. Follow the crew's instructions and wear necessary safety equipment, such as life jackets. Pay attention to weather conditions, especially during hurricane season, and be prepared for alterations or cancellations if necessary.

Boat and ferry services provide a handy and scenic form of transportation whether commuting between St. Kitts and Nevis or visiting surrounding islands. To ensure a smooth and comfortable voyage, check schedules, reserve tickets in advance where possible, and confirm departure times and destinations. Take advantage of the opportunity to explore the stunning Caribbean waters and make great memories while visiting St. Kitts and Nevis.

Traveling from St. Kitts to Nevis

Traveling between St. Kitts and Nevis is very simple and convenient, thanks to a variety of transportation choices. What you need to know about going between these two islands is as follows:

1. Inter-Island Flights: Flying between St. Kitts and Nevis is the most common and quickest way to travel. Both islands have their own airports: St. Kitts' (((International Airport Robert L. Bradshaw))) and Nevis' (((International Airport Vance W. Amory))). Daily flights between the two islands are operated by several airlines, including regional carriers. The flight lasts approximately 10 minutes and provides breathtaking aerial views of the Caribbean Sea.

2. Inter-Island boats: If you prefer a picturesque voyage and have more time on your hands, inter-island boats are a wonderful option. The ferry connects Basseterre (St. Kitts) to Charlestown (Nevis). The ferry voyage takes 45 minutes to an hour and provides stunning views of the islands and surrounding waterways. The principal operator is Sea Bridge Ferry, which has many departures throughout the day.

3. Private Boat Charters: Private boat charters are available for a more customized and flexible trip experience. You can travel between St. Kitts and Nevis by chartering a private yacht or boat. This is the best option if you want to customize your schedule while also enjoying the solitude and luxury of a private yacht. Local tour providers or yacht rental firms can help you organize private boat charters.

4. Day Trips and Excursions: If you're staying in St. Kitts or Nevis and wish to visit the other island, many tour companies provide day trips and excursions. Transportation, guided excursions to popular landmarks, and sometimes activities like snorkeling or hiking are included in these scheduled tours. It's a convenient method to see the highlights of the other island without having to plan your own transportation.

6. Customs and Immigration: Because St. Kitts and Nevis are two independent countries, you must go through customs and immigration while traveling between them. This is true whether you fly or take the ferry. Check that you have all of the appropriate travel documentation, such as a valid passport, to pass through customs and immigration.

7. Schedules and Availability: It's a good idea to double-check the schedules and availability of flights or ferry services ahead of time, especially during peak travel periods. This will assist you in planning your schedule and obtaining your preferred method of transportation. Consider booking your flights in advance to ensure availability and possibly gain better pricing.

Traveling between St. Kitts and Nevis is a lovely experience, whether you fly or ride the ferry. Because of the short distance between the islands, it is easy to explore the distinct offerings of both destinations. Regardless of your means of transportation, be prepared to appreciate the breathtaking natural beauty and friendly hospitality of St. Kitts and Nevis throughout your journey.

Apps and Websites for Travel

There are various handy travel applications and websites that can enhance your experience and make your journey more convenient while arranging a trip to St. Kitts and Nevis. Here are some suggestions:

1. Google Maps: Google Maps is a dependable and commonly used navigation program that provides precise maps, directions, and real-time traffic information. It can assist you in navigating the streets of St. Kitts and Nevis, locating nearby attractions, restaurants, and lodging, and planning your itineraries for exploring the islands.

2. Tripadvisor is a famous travel website and app that provides user-generated reviews and ratings for hotels, restaurants, sights, and activities. It can be a useful resource for researching and selecting the finest options in St. Kitts and Nevis based on other travelers' experiences and opinions.

3. Reserving.com and Expedia are excellent resources for locating and reserving rooms in St. Kitts & Nevis. They offer a variety of options, ranging from hotels to vacation rentals, as well as user ratings, images, and full information on each property. Competitive prices and simple booking procedures are frequently available.

4. Skyscanner or Kayak: These airline comparison websites and apps can help you locate the cheapest discounts on flights to St. Kitts and Nevis. They allow you to compare costs from several airlines, examine travel itineraries, and set up price alerts to track airfare fluctuations.

5. XE Currency: XE Currency is a popular currency conversion tool that offers up-to-date exchange rates. It can assist you in converting currencies and managing your budget when visiting St. Kitts and Nevis. The app also works offline, which is important when you don't have internet access.

4. Weather Apps: Knowing the weather in St. Kitts and Nevis can help you plan your activities. AccuWeather and The Weather Channel apps offer precise forecasts that include temperature, humidity, wind speed, and precipitation. They can advise you on the best times to see outdoor attractions or enjoy the beaches.

St. Kitts Tourism Authority and Nevis Tourism Authority: These official tourism websites and apps provide detailed information about the islands, including attractions, events, lodging, food options, and transportation. They're great for arranging your itinerary and getting up to date on the latest news and deals.

Ride-Hailing Apps: To book transportation in St. Kitts and Nevis, utilize popular ride-hailing apps such as Uber or Lyft. These apps let you to request rides and pay for them directly from the app, making it a convenient and dependable method to move around the islands.

Remember to download and test these applications before your travel to ensure a seamless experience. Furthermore, it's always a good idea to have a backup plan, such as offline maps or printed material, in case of technological troubles or limited internet connectivity while traveling.

CHAPTER NINE

Itinerary for 7 Days in St. Kitts and Nevis

Here is a suggested 7-day itinerary for your visit to St. Kitts & Nevis:

Day 1: Arrive in St. Kitts and check into your accommodation in Basseterre. Spend the afternoon seeing the capital city, including the UNESCO World Heritage Site Brimstone Hill Fortress National Park.

Day 2: Visit Nevis for the day. Visit Charlestown, the island's capital, then trek to the top of Nevis Peak for panoramic views of the island and the Caribbean Sea.

Day 3: Unwind on one of St. Kitts' many lovely beaches, such as Cockleshell Beach or Frigate Bay. Scuba or snorkel in the clear seas off the coast of St. Kitts.

Day 4: trip the St. Kitts picturesque Railway for a picturesque train trip. The train runs through the beautiful jungle of the island and provides breathtaking views of the shoreline.

Visit the Romney Manor Plantation and Gardens on Day 5. The manor house, which was completed in 1690, is now a museum that illustrates the story of St. Kitts' sugar production. A wide range of tropical plants and flowers can be seen in the gardens.

Day 6: Hike in St. Kitts National Park. The park has a number of hiking paths ranging from easy to difficult. In the park, you may also go horseback riding or mountain biking.

Day 7: Enjoy your final day in St. Kitts and Nevis by relaxing at the beach or pool. Have a goodbye dinner at one of the many eateries on the island.

I wish you a pleasant vacation in St. Kitts and Nevis!

Safety and Health

When visiting St. Kitts and Nevis, it is critical to prioritize your health and safety. Here are some pointers to keep you safe and healthy on your trip:

1. Consider getting travel insurance that covers medical bills, trip cancellation, and emergency evacuation before your trip. This will give you with financial security and peace of mind in the event of an unforeseen incident.

2. Medical Preparations: Before flying, check with your doctor to verify you are up to date on routine immunizations. They can also advise on any vaccines or drugs that have been

suggested for St. Kitts and Nevis, such as those for hepatitis A and B, typhoid, and malaria prophylaxis, if appropriate.

3. St. Kitts and Nevis has a tropical climate with plenty of sunshine. Wear sunscreen with a high SPF, a hat, sunglasses, and lightweight, loose-fitting clothing to protect yourself from the sun. During the warmest hours of the day, stays hydrated and seek shade.

4. Hygiene and Water Safety: Maintain appropriate hygiene habits by washing your hands with soap and water on a regular basis, or by using hand sanitizer when soap is unavailable. When it comes to water safety, it is best to drink bottled water or purified water rather than drinking tap water.

5. Mosquito Protection: St. Kitts and Nevis is in an area where mosquito-borne illnesses such as dengue fever and Zika virus can develop. Use bug repellant, wear pants, and long sleeves, and remain accommodations with screened windows or air conditioning to avoid mosquito bites. If required, consider using a bed net.

6. Precautions: While St. Kitts and Nevis are typically safe destinations, common sense precautions should be taken. Avoid walking alone at night in dimly lit or unknown areas, and keep your possessions safe. Use trustworthy

transportation providers and exercise caution when using ATMs or transporting valuables.

7. Emergency Services: Learn the local emergency phone numbers, including 911 for police and medical services. Maintain a copy of your passport, travel insurance, and critical contact information in a secure location. Seek medical attention right away if you have any health issues or an emergency.

To ensure a courteous and safe visit, it's always a good idea to keep knowledgeable about the local customs, laws, and regulations of St. Kitts and Nevis. By taking these precautions for your health and safety, you will be able to enjoy the natural beauty, cultural experiences, and friendly hospitality that St. Kitts & Nevis has to offer.

Medical Services and Facilities

Some of the medical facilities and services offered in St. Kitts and Nevis are as follows:

1. The primary hospital in St. Kitts is Joseph N. France General Hospital. It is located in the capital city of Basseterre. The hospital has a capacity of 150 beds and

provides a variety of medical services, including inpatient treatment, outpatient care, and emergency services.

2. The major hospital on Nevis is Alexandra Hospital. It's in Charlestown, the capital city. The hospital has a capacity of 50 beds and provides a wide range of medical services, such as inpatient care, outpatient care, and emergency services.

3. St. Kitts and Nevis also has a variety of private clinics and doctor's offices. These clinics provide a wide range of medical treatments such as routine examinations, minor surgery, and diagnostic tests.

4. The Ministry of Health also runs a number of health centers and clinics that provide basic medical services to St. Kitts and Nevis inhabitants. These health care facilities can be found in all of the major towns and villages on both islands.

If you require medical assistance while visiting St. Kitts and Nevis, go to the nearest hospital or clinic first. If your disease is not life-threatening, you might be eligible to see a doctor in private practice. It should be noted, however, that private doctors in St. Kitts and Nevis may not be covered by your insurance plan.

It is also a good idea to pack your own medication when visiting St. Kitts and Nevis. This is especially true if you use prescription medication. You should also keep a copy of your prescription on hand in case you need to refill your medication while on vacation.

Health Precautions and Vaccinations

Travelers to St. Kitts and Nevis should get the following vaccinations:

1. Hepatitis A is a liver infection that can be transmitted through contaminated food or water. Before visiting any underdeveloped nation, including St. Kitts and Nevis, it is a good idea to get vaccinated against hepatitis A.

2. Hepatitis B is a dangerous liver illness that can be transmitted through blood or bodily fluids. If you plan on having unprotected sex, getting a tattoo or piercing, or coming into touch with blood or body fluids in any manner, it is a good idea to get vaccinated against hepatitis B.

3. Typhoid is a bacterial infection that is spread via contaminated food or water. If you are traveling to any

developing country, including St. Kitts and Nevis, it is a good idea to get vaccinated against typhoid.

4. Yellow fever is a mosquito-borne infection that can be fatal, although it is preventable with vaccine. Yellow fever vaccination is required for visitors arriving from countries where yellow fever transmission is possible.

5. Rabies is a fatal virus that can be transmitted via a bite from an infected animal. If you are bitten by an animal in St. Kitts and Nevis, you should seek medical assistance right once.

6. Meningitis is a swelling of the membranes that surround the brain and spinal cord known as the meninges. Bacteria or viruses can cause it. There is no vaccination against viral meningitis, but there is one against bacterial meningitis. Although the bacterial type of meningitis is uncommon in St. Kitts and Nevis, it is nevertheless advisable to get vaccinated if going from a place where the disease is more frequent.

7. Dengue is a mosquito-borne sickness that causes fever, headache, muscle pain, and a rash. Although there is no dengue vaccine, there are techniques to protect yourself from mosquito bites.

8. Zika is a mosquito-borne disease that can result in birth abnormalities in kids born to infected moms. Although there is no Zika vaccine, there are techniques to protect yourself from mosquito bites.

In addition to getting vaccinated, there are a few more health measures you can take while visiting St. Kitts and Nevis:

1. Bottled water is recommended because tap water in St. Kitts and Nevis is not always safe to drink. It is recommended to drink bottled water or boiled or filtered water.

2. Avoid raw fruits and vegetables: Raw fruits and vegetables may have been infected with bacteria since they were not rinsed in clean water. It is recommended to consume cooked fruits and vegetables or fruits and vegetables that have been peeled by you.

3. Eat with caution: Avoid eating food from street sellers or restaurants with a poor sanitation record.

4.Wear long sleeves and pants to protect yourself against mosquito bites.

5. Apply insect repellent: Apply insect repellent containing DEET or Picaridin.

6. Stay informed: Check the Centers for Disease Control and Prevention (CDC) website for the most recent health risks in St. Kitts and Nevis.

Emergency Phone Numbers

Here are some emergency numbers in St. Kitts and Nevis:

St. Kitts and Nevis:

- +1 869 465-2241 for police

- Fire: +1 869 465-2515

- Call an ambulance at +1 869 465-7167.

- Contact the Coast Guard at (+1 869 465-8384).

- +1 869 466-5100 / 6892 National Disaster Management Agency

Nevis:

- +1 869 469-5344 for police

- Fire: +1 869 469-5381

- Call an ambulance at +1 869 469-5347.

- Call the Coast Guard at (+1 869 469-5422).

- +1 869 469-5411 National Emergency Management Agency

In St. Kitts and Nevis, you can also dial 911 in an emergency. 911 is North America's universal emergency number, and calls are normally routed to the nearest emergency services.

When visiting St. Kitts and Nevis, it is a good idea to maintain these emergency contacts on hand. You should also be aware of the location of the nearest hospital or clinic in case you require medical assistance.

Visitors' Safety Tips

Here are some safety precautions to take when visiting St. Kitts & Nevis:

1. Be mindful of your surroundings, especially at night when crime rates are higher. Avoid walking alone in lonely or dark regions.

2. Displaying expensive jewelry or other valuables can make you a target for theft.

3. Take caution with what you drink: Accepting drinks from strangers is dangerous since they could be laced with narcotics.

4. Don't leave anything unattended, including your luggage, cameras, and other valuables.

5. Take a taxi or take public transportation: This is a better option than walking or hitching.

6. Keep in mind the following municipal laws: Certain activities that are permitted in your home country may be prohibited in St. Kitts and Nevis.

7. Report any suspicious activity to the police: This may aid in the prevention of crime.

Here are some more safety tips for visiting St. Kitts and Nevis:

1. Keep up to date: Check the websites of the United States Department of State and the Canadian government to stay up to date on the latest crime trends and security advisories.

2. Register with your embassy or consulate so that they can contact you in an emergency.

3. Purchase a local SIM card and phone: This will allow you to call for assistance in the event of an emergency.

4. Keep a copy of your passport and other crucial documents with you: This will assist you in identifying yourself if you lose your passport or other identification documents.

5. Use your common sense: Keep an eye on your surroundings and take efforts to keep yourself safe from

Information on the Weather and Climate

Throughout the year, St. Kitts and Nevis enjoys a tropical climate with mild temperatures and heavy humidity. The average temperature during the day is 27°C (81°F) and 23°C (73°F) at night. The wet season lasts from May to December, with September and October seeing the most rain. January through April are the driest months.

Here's a more in-depth look at the weather in St. Kitts and Nevis:

1. Temperatures average 27°C (81°F) during the day and 23°C (73°F) at night.

2. The average annual rainfall is 1,200 mm (47 in).

3. September is the wettest month (250 mm / 10 inches).

4. February is the wettest month (60 mm / 2.4 inches).

5. Hurricane season lasts from June through November.

St. Kitts and Nevis has a hurricane season that lasts from June to November. Hurricanes, on the other hand, are rather uncommon in the islands. Hurricane Luis in 1995 was the most recent big hurricane to hit St. Kitts and Nevis.

If you are considering a trip to St. Kitts and Nevis, you should pack for all weather conditions. For the warm weather, bring light, comfortable clothing, as well as a rain jacket and umbrella for the rainy season. To protect yourself from the sun and insects, pack sunscreen, bug repellent, and a hat.

Travel Insurance

Travel insurance is a sort of insurance that protects you against losses that occur while you are on the road. Medical expenditures, trip cancellation or interruption, lost luggage, and other expenses may be included.

Travel insurance is not necessary for visitors to St. Kitts and Nevis, however it is recommended. The cost of travel insurance varies according to the level of coverage selected and the length of your trip.

Some of the advantages of having travel insurance include:

1. Medical expenses: Medical bills can be covered by travel insurance if you become ill or injured while traveling. This includes doctor's appointments, hospital stays, and prescription medication.

2. Vacation cancellation or interruption: If you have to cancel or interrupt your vacation due to a covered reason, such as illness, injury, or natural disaster, travel insurance can cover the cost of your trip.

3. Travel insurance can cover the expense of replacing lost luggage, including clothing, toiletries, and other personal belongings.

4. Emergency medical transportation: If you become ill or wounded while traveling, travel insurance may cover the expense of emergency medical transportation back to your home country.

5. Baggage delay: If your luggage is delayed or lost, travel insurance can cover the cost of important expenses.

If you are thinking about purchasing travel insurance, compare policies from multiple firms to discover the best coverage for your needs. You should also carefully read the policy to understand what is and is not covered.

Here are some suggestions for selecting travel insurance:

1. Compare policies from various companies: Compare rates and coverage by obtaining quotations from several different companies.

2. Read the policy thoroughly: Make sure you understand what is and is not covered.

3. Select the appropriate coverage: The level of coverage you require will be determined by your specific needs and budget.

4. Consider purchasing travel insurance as soon as you arrange your trip: this will allow you to compare policies and locate the best rate.

Check that your travel insurance covers all of your planned activities: If you intend to engage in activities not covered by your regular policy, you may need to obtain additional coverage.

CONCLUSION

As we come to the end of this St. Kitts and Nevis travel guide, it's evident that these charming Caribbean islands provide an exceptional blend of natural beauty, rich history, vibrant culture, and friendly hospitality. Whether you want to relax on gorgeous beaches, learn about history and legacy, or explore the different landscapes, St. Kitts and Nevis has something for everyone.

St. Kitts, with its vibrant capital city of Basseterre, offers an enthralling blend of colonial architecture, busy markets, and welcoming residents. From the historic Independence Square to the intriguing exhibitions at the National Museum, the island's past and present coexist together. Brimstone Hill Fortress National Park, which offers spectacular panoramic vistas, is a monument to the island's strategic importance.

The tiny sister island, Nevis, emanates a welcoming charm and calm. With its well-preserved Georgian houses and fascinating museums, the charming town of Charlestown is a refuge for history buffs. The Alexander Hamilton Museum depicts the story of one of America's founding fathers, while the Nevis Historical and Conservation Society highlights the island's diverse cultural legacy.

Nature enthusiasts will be amazed by the natural delights that St. Kitts and Nevis has to offer. Mount Liamuiga encourages daring individuals to climb its routes and be rewarded with beautiful views from the peak. The dramatic Black Rocks, the tranquil Wingfield Estate, and the lush Botanical Gardens of Nevis all provide one-of-a-kind experiences that highlight the natural beauty of the islands.

Of course, St. Kitts and Nevis' attractiveness extends beyond its land-based attractions. With their crystal-clear waters and fluffy sand, the beautiful beaches entice. From the lively South Frigate Bay Beach to the peaceful Turtle Beach, you'll discover a piece of paradise to suit your tastes. Water activities abound, from snorkeling and diving among vivid coral reefs to sailing along the shoreline and soaking up the Caribbean sun.

During your visit, you must try the local cuisine. The culinary scene in St. Kitts and Nevis is sure to delight your taste buds, from relishing the aromas of fresh fish to experiencing classic Caribbean meals flavored with native spices. Don't miss out on classic meals such as "saltfish and johnny cakes" or a delicious rum punch at a beachside bar.

You'll meet warm and welcoming residents who are proud of their background and eager to share their passion for their homeland as you explore these islands. The rhythmic sounds of calypso and soca music, the vivid costumes of carnival celebrations, and the genuine smiles of the people all add to St. Kitts and Nevis's particular character.

Remember to thoroughly plan your vacation before you go, taking into account the optimum time to visit, necessary transport arrangements, and packing requirements. Check the visa requirements and make sure you have enough travel insurance. Respect the environment and local customs while adhering to health and safety rules.

Finally, St. Kitts and Nevis provide an idyllic getaway to paradise, with breathtaking natural surroundings, a rich history, and genuine hospitality. Whether you're looking for adventure, relaxation, cultural immersion, or simply a break from regular life, these Caribbean treasures have it all. So pack your luggage, embark on a memorable adventure, and allow St. Kitts & Nevis to enchant you. Your tropical wonderland awaits you!

Printed in Great Britain
by Amazon